CATULLUS AND HORACE

CATULLUS AND HORACE

Two Poets in Their Environment

BY

TENNEY FRANK

NEW YORK

RUSSELL & RUSSELL · INC

1965

To
GRACE FRANK

CONTENTS

CATULLUS AND HORACE

I

CATULLUS AT VERONA

VERONA may recall to us Theodoric, Can Grande, Romeo and Juliet and colorful medieval romances, or the massive amphitheatre of the stolid commercial city of the Roman Empire. When Catullus was born there in 84 B.C. it was a small unkempt frontier town where barbarians of half a dozen diverse tongues gathered to barter and drink in the market place. The rustics of the neighborhood were tall husky blue-eyed Celts dressed in blankets and breeches. On market days the long-haired Raetic tribesmen, girded with dagger-belts, came down from the Alps, and the Venetic peasants plodded in with their donkey packs of wool and wheat and copper-ware. Here and there was a burly Teuton trader who had brought amber and fur and war captives all the way over the Brenner Pass to trade for wine, steel blades, glass beads and pretty scarfs, or a group of short stocky Etruscans from their mountain refuges above Lake Garda where the Celts three centuries before had driven their ancestors.

There are also a few Romans in flowing white
togas moving about through the polyglot rabble with
an air of self-assurance. These are the sons of
Roman and Italian frontiersmen who a century before, when Rome had established peace, began to
penetrate into this country. Backed by an all-
powerful government that guaranteed law and order
they had bought plantations, laid out villas, grown
rich on the abundant native labor and had taken
charge of the administration of the district. Five
years before Catullus was born Verona had been
given a town-charter by Rome and all the free-born
natives there then were declared to be "Latins."
This meant that they could vote at the town-meeting,
could legally intermarry with Romans and on election to a magistracy could become Roman citizens.
They were expected of course not to disregard the
Roman landlords when they voted. If the wild
mountaineers should raid the country or the town a
Roman magistrate was convenient to have in office,
for his word met with a quicker response from the
officers of the garrison. These Roman lords were
not as yet very numerous, and before the charter
was given they had lived quite apart from the rest
of the population. *Civis Romanus sum* meant much
in those days, and intermarriage with barbaric folk
deprived the children of such a marriage of the use

of the magic phrase. That legal barrier was removed in 89, but for the most exalted citizens a social barrier quite as effective still existed.

Among the influential Roman land-owners of the time, perhaps the most highly respected, was Catullus' father, who owned a villa on the peninsula of Sirmio which juts into Lake Garda, and he probably made his home on that garden spot. Catullus at any rate called Sirmio his home. In the fourteenth century this peninsula belonged to the magnificent Scaligers who then ruled Verona. It was in Valerius Catullus' house that Julius Caesar accepted hospitality when as proconsul of Cisalpine Gaul he stopped at Verona on his court-circuit. We may conclude that there was a town house of some pretensions as well as the farm villa, and that Valerius, like well-to-do Romans at home, was much engaged in administrative duties in the city.

There is some little doubt about the year of the birth of our poet, Gaius Valerius Catullus. A discrepancy of three years would ordinarily be of little moment, but Catullus' life was so brief that three years matter a great deal in estimating the chronology of his early poems. Here as so often we have to depend upon the confused items of St. Jerome's chronicle. Under the year "1930 post Abraham" (= 87 B.C.) Catullus' birth is recorded. Under 1959

(= 58 B.C.) is the item *Catullus XXX aetatis anno Romae moritur.* Now we know that the poet did not die in 58 because he makes four references to events of the year 55, and one to a subsequent meeting with Caesar, an event that we must date after January 1 of the year 54. The probable date of Catullus' death, as we shall see, is the spring of 54. Hence if he died at the age of thirty, the year of birth is incorrectly given, or if the year of birth is correct St. Jerome is in error regarding his age at death. We are, however, not left to an even choice between these alternatives. A man's age is frequently recorded on Roman tombstones, while the birth year is not, and that indicates which item we ought to respect. Jerome apparently fell foul of the first consulship of Cinna (87 B.C.) instead of the fourth (84 B.C.) and then reckoning thirty years from an incorrect date arrived at the erroneous date of death. This is a type of error that frequently occurs in the chronicle of St. Jerome. The dates are therefore usually accepted as being 84-54 B.C., and these satisfy all the demands of the internal evidence. Catullus was fourteen years older than Vergil. He was born nineteen years before Horace, who, therefore, was only eleven when Catullus died.

The Valerii were apparently a well-to-do family. That the poet could spend years of leisure in the

circles of the consular families at Rome, that he had
a country villa near Tivoli, and that his elder brother
travelled in Asia—doubtless on a political mission,
for such men did not engage in business—all point
to conditions of more than ordinary prosperity. The
country place on "Catullus' all-but-island, olive-
silvery Sirmio" afforded him stimulating outdoor
life, and inculcated in him a fondness for yachting
that was rare among the Romans. We cannot be
sure that "the Roman ruins where the purple flowers
grow" at the very promontory was the site of his
home, for the masonry of those ruins is apparently
of a later date. But that later villa is probably a
rebuilding of an earlier house, and its site—on the
sheer rock at the very point of the cape from which
one overlooks the cool expanse of water as far as the
snow-capped mountains behind the deep fiord of
Riva—is far more picturesque than the site of the
Scala palace at the neck of the peninsula. The Romans chose villa sites with sure taste, and the cape
is also the one point from which one has an unob-
structed reflection of both sunrise and sunset. It is
the very place from which to see his picture of the
early morning light tipping with crimson the laughing whitecaps as the early breezes stir the lake:

Post vento crescente magis magis increbescunt
Purpureaque procul nantes ab luce refulgent.

Roman though he was, growing to early youth among the decorous citizens that moved with some dignity midst the lowly subject tribes, Catullus' comportment has not precisely the Roman air. The free life, the variety of customs and manners that he saw in the town where at least six different languages were in use, the frank and blunt demeanor of the honest barbarians, chieftains and serfs, that he could watch daily, all this did not necessarily contribute to habits of austere conventionality. Catullus remains something of a savage always in his utter forthrightness. He knows no hesitation or devious turning. He loves as he hates with a violence that does not yield to discipline. He gives with the generosity of frontier hospitality, and when wounded he strikes without hesitation: his nature is as translucent as the waters of Garda. Fidelity, a virtue that counts for much among frontiersmen, is almost a religion with him, yet he is not religious in the Roman sense, had perhaps seen too many strange cults to imbibe a sure devotion to one. The Romans of Verona were not scornful of the barbaric cults. They were liberal in erecting shrines to the deities of the Celts and Raetians, sometimes identifying them with Roman gods of similar attributes, but never requiring such syncretism. Verona actually appointed regular priests in the villages within its jurisdiction for the worship of the Raetic divinities —Ihamnagalle Sqnna and Cuslanus—whoever they may have been. It is significant that the one poem of Catullus which rings with deep religious feeling is a hymn to the huntress goddess, Diana, a deity recognized at Rome, to be sure, but to him the goddess of the vast forest that lay above his home lake, a woodland goddess of the barbarous mountain tribes.[1]

> Montium domina ut fores
> Silvarumque virentium
> Saltuumque reconditorum
> Amniumque sonantum.

The Roman national cult never in a thousand years inspired such music.

Of Catullus' early education we know little. There would hardly be proficient lecturers in a small frontier town like Verona, but a man like Valerius would probably bring a tutor for his boys from Rome. Ordinarily such a tutor would be expected first of all to teach his pupils to read and speak Greek, to do their arithmetic, and to study Greek and Latin literature, beginning with Homer and Ennius. If the student were to go into public life, as gentlemen were expected to do, he must take a severe course in the Greek and Roman orators, learning the rules of rhetoric and writing an abundance of practical exercises. A course in philosophy would round out his education. It is not likely that Catullus reached his final examinations, though the scant references to his education leave us in some doubt. He knew his Greek well and had read rather widely though it is likely that much of his browsing was done in Rome. In a letter written on a later visit to Verona (68 a) he mentions the lack of books of a romantic type there except for the one case which he had brought along. The fact that he had played at verse-writing from his boyhood, and that too in the meters that were popular in Alexandria seems to indicate that his tutor had put him in touch with the newer Greek poets. Yet he knew Sappho, at least soon after reaching Rome, at a time when the old Greek bards were not generally read in Rome. There are few traces of the old Roman poets in him, though some scholars wish to infer that an occasional resemblance to Lucretius should be taken as proof that Ennius is a common source of these two. It is more plausible that Catullus was allowed to read some of Lucretius in manuscript in his last year. That Catullus ever completed an advanced course in rhetoric and philosophy is unlikely. Perhaps his purpose in going to Rome was to enter on these studies in order to perfect himself for public life, but as we know Rome soon drew him into other more

enticing distractions. It was as well. Neither
rhetoric nor philosophy had anything to contribute
to a poet of his temper.

Most of his boyhood verses were probably destroyed, but we have at least one jocular lampoon
(no. 17) in priapean meter which belongs to the
north. It scolds an old dullard for not keeping a
watchful eye on his pretty young wife. It is freely
colloquial, as befits the theme, runs with a tripping
lilt, and reveals the facility in artless effects which is
always evident in his limpid verse. There is also
an indifferent bit of home gossip written in Alexandrian elegiac couplets (67) which may belong to
this period, but I should infer that it was written
during a later visit home when we know that he was
experimenting with this form. It does not flow with
the same ease as the trifling verse which he played
with before he went to Rome and which came so
readily to his pen when he began to write to Clodia.

We have not the date of Catullus' departure for
Rome, but it was probably in 62, when he was
twenty-two years of age.[2] He seems to have escaped
the excitement of the Catilinarian conspiracy in 63
but not wholly its consequences. The urban praetor
of that year was a pompous noble of a very old
family, Q. Caecilius Metellus Celer. His wife was
Clodia, the Lesbia of Catullus' poems. This praetor

was a reliable conservative, and as he had drawn the lot to become governor of Cisalpine Gaul for the next year, he was hurried north when the Catilinarian rebellion broke out, with the powers of proconsul and an army of three legions for the purpose of blocking the passage of the rebel army if it should attempt to retreat northward. Catiline was defeated in January by the consular army before Metellus was involved, but Metellus remained in his province for the year 62 as was his duty, in order to guard the frontier and hold court in the towns of the province. He must have visited Verona on his circuit and he was probably the guest of Catullus' father while there, as was Caesar, his successor. It is just possible that Clodia visited the province with her husband and thus met Catullus at his home, but it is not likely. The governor's circuit was not a tourist's excursion. It is more likely that Catullus secured from Metellus letters of introduction to his wife and friends at Rome. At any rate it is certain that Catullus came to Rome during the year, if not before, and that it was Clodia and her circle of friends that he came to know very early during his sojourn at the capital.

In 62, Catullus was only twenty-two years of age; Clodia [8] was probably ten years older. He was an unknown provincial, and provincials were usually very, very insignificant at Rome; she bore one of the oldest names of Rome: the Claudian name was inscribed on the bronze code of the twelve tables four centuries before, on the arches of the first aqueduct, on the milestones of the first Appian way, and a goodly score of times on the august consular lists. It is difficult in these days of democracy to imagine the pompous staccato with which a Claudius or a Metellus would chop off his patronizing salutation to a youthful Transpadane like Catullus, or in turn the tremor of awe with which a Catullus was expected to return such a greeting. When Catullus brought his letter of introduction all the way up that steep ramp behind the Castor temple to the conspicuous palace of the proconsul it is not likely that he expected to be invited to call again, much less to find Clodia all graciousness and eager to listen to his embarrassed sentences. We know how he felt as he sat before the woman whom all Rome called beautiful, listening to her soft laughter, feeling his very wits deserting him:

> Qui sedens adversus identidem te
> spectat et audit
> dulce ridentem—misero quod omnis
> eripit sensus mihi.

He had no words of his own that could express this new sensation; of all the poets he had read no one had put it adequately into words. In Sappho he found a poem that he might make his own, if he could translate it and put himself in the place of the lover for whom Sappho spoke. And so he did, but of course he could not then have dared imagine that he might ever send it. Clodia lived on the Palatine by right of all that was great at Rome, and he was a mere Transpadane.

Clodia's manner was not conventional. She had suffered much before she became the wife of Metellus. Her father had been banished by Cinna during the civil wars and had then lost his property. Though restored by Sulla and given an important governorship which brought a restitution of his position and some property, he died in 76 B.C. leaving his large family of three sons and three daughters in straitened circumstances. Without parental care and advice, with the needs of station unsatisfied by scanty means, the children apparently learned to devise a life of their own. The eldest daughter had married Marcius, the consul of 68, before the worst disaster, and the youngest had married Lucullus, whose long absence in the Asiatic wars ended with a divorce as soon as he returned. The younger brother Clodius grew reckless from trying to make a position for himself by hook or crook, winning thereby a name for dare-deviltry. Our Clodia, the second daughter, though famous for her wit and beauty, married less well and apparently at a later age than her sisters. To have a father in high office of state and a goodly dower which might aid a husband in a long career of civil service without pay counted for much in that closed senatorial society, but Clodia had neither. This fact is of some significance in comprehending her later career. The pressure of social expectations in the face of poverty may also account for the nervous and erratic behavior of her brother, Clodius, his attempts to win favor by cheap methods while serving with his brother-in-law Lucullus in Asia, his uncertain attitude during the Catilinarian conspiracy, and his desertion of his party to become a radical tool of Caesar in 59. Clodia's life could not have been normal during those years of difficulty. She read much in an age when literature was made for men, and she took an interest in her younger brother's ambitions and acquired a taste for political intrigue, both of which brought her into the company of men of the world.

Her husband, Metellus Celer, though of good family was not, like herself, a patrician. His political prejudices were correct and reliable, and in addition he could profit from the friendship and aid of the magnificent Pompey to whom he was related by marriage. He was in fact generally considered in line for the consulship. For our estimate of him we need not depend wholly upon a stinging verse of Catullus—who in the circumstances might well have kept silent—but we possess a blunt letter [4] written by the man himself to Cicero early in 62 B.C. It happened that Cicero on laying down his consulship had had a bitter passage of words with Metellus' brother. Metellus undertakes to rebuke Cicero. The heavy sarcasm, the childish threats of political retribution, the crude comparison of his own lofty station with Cicero's lack of ancestry become conspicuous in the light of Cicero's exquisitely phrased reply. Even later after the two men were reconciled, Cicero speaks of Metellus as "a desert waste." He was hardly a companion for a Clodia, and we are not surprised to find a year later that Cicero refers to quarrels in the household: seditiosa (referring to Clodia) cum viro bellum gerit.

II

CATULLUS AND CLODIA

It would be hazardous to attempt a description of Clodia, though it means much that Cicero, despite his hatred of her, constantly refers to her lustrous eyes, and to the troop of brilliant young men of Rome who hovered about her. Catullus does not speak of her beauty as frequently as one might expect, but this was before the days of the troubadours when lips and eyelashes and throats became the subject of verse. And even when he does, as in assertions like this (86), who would accept him as a witness? "They call Quintia beautiful? I'd say fair, and straight, and tall, but not beautiful. There's no wit or grace in all her bulk. Lesbia is beautiful, loveliness absolute, thieving all charm from all."

Catullus, the shy, inexperienced youth from the country, fell very deeply in love with this woman. To comprehend the first genuine love lyrics of ancient poetry one must understand the situation that made them possible or mistake their real flavor. They are not the pretty verse exercises of the sophisticated Greeks, nor do they breathe the morbid

17

eroticism of Propertius. Catullus did not write these
first poems for Clodia. She was still to him a far-
away princess. How often in his country home had
he read of the great Claudian nobles, in the volumes
of Fabius, Ennius and Cato, themselves great men
of an heroic day! Now roaming about in the rabble
of the Forum he could actually look up the steep
cliffs of the Palatine to the palace where a Clodia
lived—a woman of that race who had actually
deigned to talk to him. There can be little doubt
that his first verse was that translation of Sappho
(51). The substance of it is:

> Like a god is he who beholds thee and hears
> thy soft laughter: ah me, it has bereft me of my
> senses. When I beheld thee, Lesbia, my voice
> failed me, my tongue was dumb, a flame pierced
> me, my ears confused all words, a cloud closed
> my eyes.

Sappho had written two stanzas more, but they were
too literal to express his love. It was not his trem-
bling body that he cared to recall. It was the be-
wilderment of soul that startled him and that he
wished to write out for himself, and so he proceeds
in his own words, futilely:

> It is idleness that ails thee, Catullus, the law-
> less, uncontrolled wanting. It has destroyed
> greater than thee.

It was noticed long ago that this can safely be considered the first of the Lesbia poems. In all his verses he calls Clodia, Lesbia, a name suggested of course in translating this poem of Sappho's. Catullus indeed uses the Sapphic meter twice only, here and in his acrid farewell to Clodia seven years later (no. 11). The meter of the latter is contrived to recall the first poem, and what is more significant—as Mackail has noticed—the rare word *identidem*, so expressively used in line three of the first, is placed with biting force in the same position of the stanza in the latter one, and nowhere else in Catullus does the word occur.

Catullus was, of course, not aware that in making this adaptation of Sappho he was writing what we now consider the first modern love lyric—though it would be bold to offer a complete interpretation of Sappho's words. This is one of the numerous instances where criticism fails for want of biography.[5] Her verses are addressed by her to one of the girls in her "school." The girl is apparently about to leave, probably to be married. Sappho begins as though speaking of the lover who is to marry the girl, and of his supreme happiness when he beholds his bride and hears her laughter. However, when Sappho presently writes of the physical expression of the emotion caused by the girl, she drops into the first person, and seems purposely to have hidden the transition. Critics do not agree on the exact meaning of her words. Perhaps she intends to convey vicariously, as it were, what she is persuaded the bridegroom's love must be, or it may be that she has lost herself wholly in her own emotion, or there may be hidden in the lines a deep sense of her own anticipated loss in consequence of the impending departure. "Longinus," who has preserved the poem for us, calls it a "concourse of all passions." "Longinus," who knew more about Sappho than we do, should have told us what he meant by that. At any rate Sappho's poem could not in the nature of the case be a song of a lover to his beloved. In the revolutions that followed Sappho's day, the Greek world shifted the axis of society. Men now constituted all of society that counted and men wrote of men for men. There was nothing in that life to beget love lyrics, and a convention was created in literature which had not yet been broken in Catullus' day, even though the new Hellenic and especially Roman society was almost ready for a more romantic self-expression. Catullus was of course not aware that he was breaking conventions. He was deeply in love and he found nothing in poetry that would express what he felt. The poem of Sappho would suffice if he could eliminate its complexity and could speak in his own person for himself. This he did. He is the lover and the speaker too, and so for the first time in ancient verse the lover sings of his love without hesitation; the fetters of a literary convention have been broken.

In much of Catullus' verse we are aware of a pagan directness, a lack of the spiritual restraint that romantic verse of a Christian epoch has taught us to expect. The striking thing is that Catullus himself felt this lack in Sappho's verse, and, checking himself before the fourth stanza, ended so strangely off the tonic of Sappho's poem. We need not misunderstand this hesitancy. Catullus was completely a pagan. But if Christianity has given richness and depth to romance, perhaps it has done so by imposing a restraint upon passion that gives it time to find imaginative utterance. To Catullus, Lesbia in these early days was more remote than the most exalted *princesse lointaine.* There were mountains of splendor and majesty and history between him and her— and, to be realistic, there were years, and a proconsular husband. Catullus was too dazzled to enter into the vaguest of suppositions that a Clodia could possibly requite his love. This, perhaps, explains the romance that pervades his earlier verses. Much later, when he did not quite understand how to analyze his first emotions, he naïvely spoke of his early love for Clodia as being as pure and simple as filial devotion. The simile was not quite correct, but his experience had somewhat exceeded the pagan vocabulary of the day.

What Clodia thought of the impulsive young fellow we can hardly surmise. Perhaps she merely bade him call again with the natural grace of her class and was surprised to find him when he came. Perhaps she found him a relief after the pompous society of her consular neighbors: Cicero, Crassus and the haughty Lutatius Catulus. How far she had acquired a reputation for coquetry at this time we cannot say. Perhaps she needed his aid in her political intrigues, for her troublesome younger brother was again at his escapades and required all the enticing influence of his sister to save him from political annihilation.

It was in December of the year 62, when Metellus was still in his province, that Clodius—always eager for forbidden fun—secreted himself in Caesar's house while the secret rites of the "Good Goddess" were being performed by the matrons of noble families. He was discovered, and the priests demanded exemplary punishment for the profanation of holy rites. Had his father lived Clodius probably would have been put on a meager allowance and sent abroad for a year or two. It did not mend matters that Caesar seized the opportunity for divorcing his wife because she had permitted sacrilege in the house of the pontifex maximus. "Caesar's wife should be above suspicion," he explained—Caesar himself was not always above canting. The staid senators demanded a trial. The penitent miscreant went the rounds and begged for pity; Clodia, more practical, called in her young worshippers and bound them to promises of direct aid. There were several brilliant young men about town, some who had even participated in the parlor socialism of the Catilinarian clique, who were more or less in sympathy with the rakish pranks of Clodius. They could at least hoot and jeer at the trial. Curio, a boon companion of Mark Antony, promised to undertake the defense, while Calvus,⁶ a fiery young lawyer and poet—known today chiefly because of his friendship for Catullus —undertook to assist. What part Catullus was asked to play we do not know—perhaps it was he who had brought his skilful friend Calvus to aid in the defense.

Four exciting months were spent in the shrewdest of political moves. It is amusing to watch the august senators of Rome squabbling over this trifling matter. The charge, of course, was sacrilege and a special court must be organized and a special jury panel drawn. Clodius secured the aid of a tribune who vetoed every move until a bill was drawn to his satisfaction, and Hortensius, who was supposed to be the whip in the senate, accepted the compromise, not without suspicion of yielding to undue influence. Metellus had returned home from Gaul meanwhile, and was attempting to draw Clodia out of the unseemly fray. But she was enjoying herself, and Cicero, who lived across the street, had cause to know that there were unhappy scenes in her house. It was May before the trial finally came off. Curio rested his case on an alibi, but unfortunately Cicero, an observing neighbor, stated when called to the witness stand that Clodius had been seen in the city on the day in question. Cicero in giving an account of the trial to his friend, Atticus, adds that the jury would have voted for conviction had not Calvus sent in a servant to the jury with bribes and promises that involved the good name of "certain women." Later he is more explicit and names Clodia. By this time, however, Cicero was rather excited, and it is quite possible that he made remarks to his discreet friend which he would not have cared to make in court. For him the case might prove disastrous, since Clodius had threatened to get his revenge by attacking the legality of Cicero's execution of the Catilinarians. In fact three years later Clodius sprang the trap and Cicero was exiled. Cicero realized his danger from the beginning, and fear colors all his remarks about Clodius and his sister.

The acquittal of Clodius in May, 61 was only the end of the first act in a long series of political intrigues in which Clodia played an active part. The plot of the second act was so labyrinthine that Metellus was somehow induced to subscribe to bills that he later had to repudiate. Only Clodia could have accomplished this. In point of fact Clodius had decided to vault into control of the popular party. Caesar was now absent as proconsul of Spain, Pompey, who had called himself a democrat before going to the Mithridatic war, had just returned and was expected to shape the policies of the popular party by the mere weight of his magnificence, but Clodius was shrewd enough to see that Pompey was too ponderous to succeed as a party leader. The only way to leap ahead of Caesar would be to divest himself of his patrician status—a very unusual sacrifice of dignity—so as to get the plebeian office of tribuneship by means of which he might control the popular assembly. Metellus was in fact lured into signing the bill for the first step, but was warned in time and retreated. Clodius worked desperately and brought his bill up again and again. There must have been many caucuses in Clodia's house to which her husband was not invited.

Plutarch, who was a Greek and unaccustomed to women in politics, is quite perturbed by Clodia's activity at this time. He naïvely concludes, for instance, that Cicero's visits to Clodia implied a love affair. But although Clodia's manner may have been unconventional, there was nothing unusual in her participation in the political counsels of her family. One has only to recall the salon of Cornelia where the policies of the Gracchi were discussed, or of her granddaughter Sempronia where the young radicals used to meet who later supported Catiline, or of women like Servilia, Porcia, and Tertulla who participated in the political plans of Brutus and Cassius and at times made the decisive proposals. The society of Rome was a ruling aristocracy in which all the combined influences of families, of the wealth, brains and loyalties that could be called into service by men and women were pooled, as it were, to aid the members of the family to secure positions of ancestral dignity. Clodia's crime in the eyes of Roman society was not her desertion of the loom, but her support of her heterodox brother against the respectable party of her stodgy husband. That she discovered the value of lustrous eyes in furthering her political pleas may be accepted as at least plausible. That the conservatives gave voice to the charge is not surprising, since Metellus had now been elected to the consulship and had thereby elevated Clodia to the highest dignity a woman could reach. Her palace would now be frequented by staid old leaders of the state who had hesitated to mingle with the young radicals visiting there in the past.

All these comings and goings probably left the door open for Catullus. He met Clodia frequently, and this did not contribute to his peace of mind. He soon learned to see her as she was, not a more-than-human lady of an ancient line, but a clever, coquettish woman who smiled her devotees into obedience. He loved her none the less intensely for that, but his love was coming down from the mountain tops. Among her whimsical words and gestures he searched for any proof of requital. If it happened that, while conversing with him, she played with her pet finch, he imagined that she was seeking to distract her mind from the pains of love.

> Et solaciolum sui doloris,
> credo, ut tum gravis adquiescat ardor.

One cannot turn surmise into certainty; even Catullus only ventures a "credo." But Clodia must at least have been aware of his passion, and there had been some sort of comment upon his visits (83):

Lesbia berates me when her husband is by— which pleases the simpleton. You dolt, this is

only a proof of her love. If she could forget
me she would be silent.

But (in 92) Catullus is still arguing himself into a
conviction of which he is none too sure.

Lesbia must love me, for she speaks ill of me;
I know, for in my very imprecations I love her.

These conceits are not very inspiring poetry, but they
are of use in tracing the course of an obscure plot.
They bring us to a period sometime after Metellus'
return from the north and before his death in March
59, and they reveal, as we have assumed above, the
lapse of time that was necessary before Catullus
could bring himself to earth, and before he and
Clodia ceased to speak to each other in riddles.

Catullus' circle of friends at Rome grew very
rapidly, and many of them belonged to the nobility
where we should hardly expect a young provincial to
find such a ready welcome. The only adequate explanation of this fact is of course his early acquaintance with Clodia. It is in the "occasional" verse
thrown off in letters of thanks to these friends, in
invitations, in missives of rapid comment that we
recognize the impulsive generosity of this young
poet. Two young men, Veranius and Fabullus, not
otherwise known to us, are mentioned several times.
It seems that they had been with Caesar in Spain and

that later they went on the staff of Caesar's father-
in-law, Piso, to Macedonia.   These letters are useful in fixing certain dates in the poet's career.   Since
Catullus knew them before they went he must have
been in Rome in 62.   On their return—Caesar came
back in July 60—Catullus greets Veranius with exuberant lines (9) which it would be easier to match
in modern Italian verse than in the language of
Cicero:

> adplicansque collum
> iocundum os oculosque saviabor;
> O quantumst hominum beatiorum,
> quid me laetius est beatiusve?

To Fabullus there is a versified invitation (13)
which is cast in the form of a poem by Philodemus
(Anth. Pal. XI, 44).   Since Philodemus, like Fabullus, was attached to Piso, the reminiscence is not surprising.   Catullus apparently intended his friend to
recognize his verse as an adaptation of Philodemus'
epigram.   That this Greek poet-philosopher so early
influenced Catullus is interesting, for Vergil and
Horace also owed much to him.[7]   We shall meet
him again in a poem that is less flattering.

Calvus, the lawyer and poet, became Catullus'
boon-companion, and by later writers the two men
are almost always mentioned in one breath.   Calvus
was the son of Licinius Macer, a man who was par-

ticularly known for his anti-aristocratic History of
Rome. The young man (Licinius Macer Calvus)
was about the same age as Catullus, a trifle too young
to be involved in the Catilinarian revolution, but,
as we have seen, ripe for some participation in the
Clodian affair. Though fiery and nervous in temper,
he had by careful training acquired a studiously
matter-of-fact style. Fifteen years later when
Cicero wrote his history of Roman oratory in order
to justify his own florid and expansive style he took
special pains to point out what he called the in-
adequacies of Calvus' manner of speech.[8] We know
now that Cicero's criticism was in fact a tribute to a
rival and a confession of fear. Calvus, who felt
that senatorial copiousness was out of date in a day
of quick action and realism in politics, had frankly
adopted the manner of Lysias as more effective than
that of the Hellenistic orators and he called himself
an Atticist. It was not he who introduced the new
theory into Rome, but it was he more than any except Caesar who revolutionized Roman prose under
the very eyes of the great Cicero. The first time
we hear of his participation in affairs is in the trial of
Clodius, though not there as a speaker. It is in 58,
during the intense political battles daily waged in
the forum, that we find him taking a vigorous part
against the tools of Caesar, the new political boss of

Rome. And in such battles he had the ready aid of Catullus' biting epigrams. But to that we must return later.

If Calvus made Catullus something of an anti-Caesarian pamphleteer, it was probably Catullus who turned Calvus to writing verses. So closely associated were these two men in style and manner, whether in writing love elegies, lampoons or romantic epics, that later critics always associated their names. Calvus' political lampoons doubtless contained little of poetic beauty, to judge from the few quotations that have survived, but they would help us greatly in interpreting the spirit of Rome's most intense political conflict. His epyllia long found favor. Written in the Alexandrian fashion, they exhaled that mist of romance that Horace labored so hard to dispel. Calvus also wrote occasional verse and some love lyrics that were sung in Horace's day, as well as a poem unique in Roman literature—a long elegy to Quintilia, his wife, after her death. It speaks well of the man that he comprehended and loved Catullus. We have some verses of Catullus (50) scribbled off at fever heat after an exciting evening spent with him over the cups and tablets— when they had thrown off lampoons and epigrams at high speed. Some of those very exercises may have been rescued from Catullus' scrap-book for the odd collection that we have. It is not poetry of a high order, but it gives a glimpse of a Roman evening when the world was young, and it may be read as an antidote to Cicero's speeches of the same period.

Catullus also met Cicero, as we learn from a letter of thanks which must be discussed later. Indeed he could hardly have escaped the observant eye of the ex-consul whose splendid palace stood opposite the poet's favorite haunt. But Cicero spares Catullus in his vituperations of Clodia. He had a weakness for young literary men, and was soon to become a favorite of the "unshaved" young rebels when Caesar's autocratic control frightened them out of the popular party.

It is more difficult at first sight to comprehend what bond of sympathy there could have been between the aristocratic orator Hortensius, now about fifty-five years of age, and the young provincial of twenty-four. And yet it is he who consoles the poet when he needs consolation and advises him to find distraction in translating from the Greek romances. It is possible that their friendship arose indirectly through Clodia. A letter [9] of Cicero written to Atticus in 60 begins thus: "I can give you good news I think. Valerius was acquitted, defended by Hortensius. It is generally thought that the acquittal was due to the influence of Afranius, but I suspect

as you do that Pompey has been enjoying himself.
. . . We shall find out when you return." This is
very enigmatical, but the Valerius in question may
be Valerius Catullus. Since Nepos, our poet's friend,
was a particular friend of Atticus the acquittal may
have concerned him. The "enjoyment" would then
have reference to Clodia's intrigues in behalf of the
poet. Atticus might on his return get the facts from
Clodia for he met her frequently. If Hortensius
took Catullus' case at Clodia's urging, this fact would
explain the old lawyer's personal interest in him a
year later.

Asinius Pollio, known chiefly for his literary work
during the Augustan period, was another early acquaintance. A brief epigram (no. 12) belonging to
about 60 B.C. mentions Asinius intimately, though the
boy was then only about sixteen years of age. Catullus had had some young men in to dine, among them
Marrucinus, Pollio's brother, who, by way of a
prank, had slipped one of the Spanish napkins into
his pocket as a souvenir of a memorable occasion.
Catullus sends a lampoon to fetch it back, and mentions incidentally the better manners of his gentle-
manly young brother. This is of course the first
time that Pollio is referred to in literature, and it
is interesting to find that even in his school days he
was so well known to Catullus, for later when he

became a distinguished poet, orator, historian and critic the influence of Catullus and Calvus was very potent in his work. He was in fact one of the important links between the Catullian and the Horatian groups.

To these friends of Catullus we shall presently have to add Cinna, the poet, Memmius, the patron of Lucretius, Cornificius, the orator, Furius Bibaculus, the satirist, Valerius Cato, a critic who did much to shape the taste of the day in favor of the younger group, and others as well. It is remarkable how at Rome, where social lines were usually demarked with care and literary cliques were painfully exclusive, Catullus seems to have walked across all barriers with absolute freedom. Clodia probably knew the reason why.

Metellus was now consul, presiding stupidly over a senate that broke under his hopeless leadership. It was the last year of the free republic, for Caesar came home in July and formed the "first triumvirate." Thirty years later when Pollio wrote the history of the downfall of the republic he began with the consulship of Metellus. Had the consul been a man of some imagination a few obvious moves could have kept the senators and knights together in an effective bloc, and would have saved Pompey and Crassus from the enticements of Caesar. But

Metellus was intransigent, and hammered away with outworn party-phrases that drove the last wedge between the factions. To make his harried life even more distracting the news came that Ariovistus was creating havoc in Gaul and that the Helvetians were about to march westward. These Germans served Caesar a good turn more than once. Metellus was chosen by the senate to march into Gaul to defend the "allies of the Roman people." He was, however, in no great hurry to go. He called for a levy to be sure, and he sent envoys into Gaul, but he himself delayed. Perhaps he thought that the senate could not endure without him. At any rate he still kept Clodius from the tribuneship, thus playing Caesar's game again, and annoying his wife not a little.

It seems to have been during this year, when Clodia was officially the foremost lady of Rome, that Catullus told her what he had now found the courage—or the encouragement—to say. The poems that he now wrote her are too well known to require repetition. They do not imply that his love was unrequited. He had no doubts, and he was not now musing to himself alone when he wrote:

> Vivamus, mea Lesbia, atque amemus,
> rumoresque senum severiorum
> omnes unius aestimemus assis.

> Soles occidere et redire possunt:
> nobis cum semel occidit brevis lux,
> nox est perpetua una dormienda.

Or if one could possibly doubt that this poem was sent to her, the seventh, which followed closely, is decisive:

> Quaeris quot mihi basiationes
> tuae, Lesbia, sint satis superque . . .

Needless to say, a consul's palace is hardly the place for such themes. As to what followed, we have only stray hints to piece together in uncertain order. A part of the story is hypothetical, depending upon the correct identification of cryptonyms in the mysterious 68th poem of Catullus and upon the interpretation of allusions in Cicero's defence of Caelius against Clodia's prosecution in the year 56. Caelius Rufus [10] now enters the story. He was a clever, well-educated and very handsome youth a few years older than Catullus. After the Catilinarian conspiracy, in which he had burned his fingers, his father had sent him to his African plantation for a year to brood over his sins. When Caelius returned to Rome—apparently in the year 60—he was ready to enter upon the preliminaries of a political career by taking cases in court. He also wanted to rent a conspicuous house in the fashionable quarters of Rome. Clodius, his old friend, let one to him, on the Palatine, and this house happened to be near Clodia's.[11] Caelius became a good friend of Catullus as well as of Clodia and introduced the young poet to Manlius Torquatus, a member of the liberal nobility, who dabbled in poetry, law and Epicurean philosophy. It seems that Catullus at this time was no longer welcome at the house of Metellus, and if the repetition of *candidiore nota* in two poems (68 and 107) is intentional, the temporary separation was due to Clodia's own decision. But it could not have lasted long. Manlius was appealed to. Even a consul's wife could enter his house,[12] and on a certain eventful day Catullus was there, listening for the footfall that he dared not hope to hear. Then Lesbia appeared.

"Thither came my fair goddess with silent footfall,
    I saw one gleaming foot upon the threshold,
    I heard the rasp of her sandal; there she stood."

Quel giorno più non vi leggemmo avante. This is the day to which he keeps recurring later. Were there no more like it? There are in any case few poems to Lesbia which can with certainty be referred to the months that followed that day.

III

MISER CATULLE

CAESAR took office as consul in January 59 and it was soon apparent that he was master of Rome and would rule with an iron hand. The senate was helpless. The consul had bound the knights by a promise of favorable contracts and had won over Pompey—his only possible rival—by promising the general that his soldiers should have the bonus in lands which he had pledged them but had thus far failed to secure. Cicero was kept at arm's length by threats of letting Clodius have his revenge, and Clodius was kept out of the tribunate till after Caesar's ascendancy had been completely acknowledged. Clodia by this time had probably lost some of her interest in politics. The young rebels of the Curio-Calvus group were drifting toward Cicero, forsaking Clodius who had nothing to offer; why should they support him in his futile bluster against a more futile nobility? They began to comprehend that Caesar and (as it seemed for the moment) Pompey were the masters and likely to remain so. In that case there would no longer be free opportunities

for young men to rise to high offices of state except
at the beck and call of these two princes. Through
the first months of the year they floundered about
bewildered. Then they began to turn to Cicero for
leadership since he alone had proved capable of unit-
ing the parties that could form an effective bloc
against the Catilinarian democracy. Curio, who had
acted as counsel for Clodius and had attacked
Cicero's testimony two years before, now flattered
and cajoled him, hoping that he would act. But
these young men hardly realized how effectively
Cicero had been trapped. The young poets began
a campaign of lampooning against Caesar and Pompey that did not hesitate at vitriolic scurrility. Calvus used untranslatable phrases in his skits deriding
Pompey for his submission to Caesar. Memmius
raked up the blackest gossip to hurl at Caesar.
Furius Bibaculus took his fling at both. The political
epigrams of Catullus are perhaps the most bitter,
though those that have survived seem to date from
the years following. However, it is not likely that
he deserted his friends at this crisis.

Catullus' friendship for Cicero—shared with the
others of his group—is attested by a handsome letter
of thanks for some unknown service. We cannot
date the letter but it may well belong to this period
when Cicero was in high esteem with the group and

was in fact eager for their friendship because of possible attacks to come:

> Disertissime Romuli nepotum,
> Quot sunt quotque fuere, Marce Tulli,
> Quotque post aliis erunt in annis,
> Gratias tibi maximas Catullus
> Agit, pessimus omnium poeta,
> Tanto pessimus omnium poeta
> Quanto tu optimus omnium patronus.

Several editors have attempted to find sarcasm in these generous lines.[18] I cannot see how any reader of Catullus could suspect the sincerity of his over-modest designation of himself as *pessimus poeta*. Catullus did not yet consider himself a serious poet. His dedicatory poem proves that. As for Cicero's casual disparagement of the "new poets" in his Tusculans, that statement appeared many years after this when both Catullus and Calvus were dead and only inferior members of the group were writing. The point usually stressed is that "optimus omnium patronus" is capable of a double meaning, since *omnium* may be connected either with *optimus* or with *patronus*. But it is an anachronism to suggest that during Catullus' lifetime Cicero could have been accused at Rome of carelessness in the choice of his clients. To be sure we do not know the occasion that would call for an expression of gratitude, but the two had many mutual friends and must have met. Perhaps Cicero had written one of his generous letters of recommendation to his brother Quintus, the governor of Asia, in favor of Catullus' brother in Asia, or perhaps he had secured him that position on the staff, or passed on to Quintus instructions from Catullus at the death of his brother. Guesses are of small consequence. My only purpose is to suggest the close relationship between these men. The important point is that during Caesar's consulship the group of young men to which Catullus and Calvus belonged drew very close to Cicero in a common fear of the triumvirate.

It was probably in this year of disasters (59 B.C.) that Catullus received a grievous blow in the news that his brother, whom he loved devotedly, had died near Troy in Asia. As we have remarked, Cicero's brother, Quintus, was then governor of Asia—had in fact gone to the post in 61—and since Catullus moved in the circles of the political nobility and not of the knights we may assume that his brother was not engaged in business ventures in the province but rather that he had accompanied Quintus there as staff officer. Catullus' grief on hearing of his brother's death was very deep. We have the epitaph which he wrote (101), apparently when he later visited the tomb. I cannot find a translation

that does not blur the pain and dim the sincerity of
the inimitable lines.   Fortunately it is too well-
known to need English words.

Multas per gentes et multa per aequora vectus
   Advenio has miseras, frater, ad inferias,
Ut te postremo donarem munere mortis
   Et mutam nequiquam adloquerer cinerem,
Quandoquidem fortuna mihi tete abstulit ipsum,
   Heu miser indigne frater adempte mihi.
Nunc tamen interea haec prisco quae more parentum
   Tradita sunt tristi munere ad inferias,
Accipe fraterno multum manantia fletu,
   Atque in perpetuom, frater, ave atque vale.

Nor does its simple limpidity want or endure comment.

At that moment of distress his parents needed him
and he went home to Verona.   He received letters
of consolation from his friends, and Hortensius made
the practical suggestion that he absorb his thoughts
in writing, and that he might attempt translating
some poem of Callimachus.   In time Catullus did
try to convert into Callimachean Latin the somewhat
over-famous Coma Berenices (66)—a whimsical and
artificial piece of Alexandrian court flattery.   But he
was hardly satisfied with the subject or with his
partial success.   And in the versified epistle (65)
which he sends with his version he speaks with feeling of his inability to write under stress of sorrow,

and adds that he produced the translation only to prove that he was grateful for Hortensius' thoughtfulness in suggesting it. It was indeed strange advice for a staid old orator to give, and it was far from the best. Alexandrian euphuism might well be counted on to destroy Catullus' lucid and direct style. But there was a tradition that "minor verses" were not dignified and that a poet must prove his qualities in sustained verse narration. The advice shows that Hortensius at least recognized that Catullus was a poet.

It is probable that Catullus also wrote the sixty-seventh poem at this time, an involved and obscure monologue of a door blurting out the secrets of its household. The characters involved are ostensibly Veronese but the model of the poem seems to have been Alexandrian. In both of these poems Catullus was trying to acquire a new style but it proved to be one little suited to his pen.

From Manlius also, who apparently did not know the reason for his absence, came an elegiac epistle asking for verses. Manlius was unhappy—apparently his light-of-love was no more—and like Hortensius urged Catullus to paraphrase some Greek erotic epyllion for him. Then he added—and this may have been the real purpose of the missive—that Catullus would do well to return, since Clodia was

enjoying herself with other suitors. The reference
was to Caelius, it would seem, though Catullus did
not at the time know who his rival was. If our
chronology is correct Metellus was now dead, and
Clodia was finding distraction at the fashionable resort at Baiae near Naples. Catullus attempted to
reply—in the first forty lines of the poem (68),
which he presently rejected. This is a disheveled
epistle [14] in couplets, written in a confusion of mixed
emotions: a sharp refusal to discuss Clodia—though
his words betray the fact that the news was not
wholly unexpected; an avowal that because of his
brother's death he is not in a mood to write the verses
that Manlius requests, and a statement that he did
not have the requisite books at Verona for such work.
The lines are prosaic except those which refer to his
brother.

This epistle of refusal was apparently never sent,
for we find following it another longer epistle
(68 b) which actually grants the request for verses,
and this later poem repeats the five best lines of the
earlier one. There is no other instance of such a
repetition and it is hardly explicable except on the
theory that the first draft was suppressed. Most
critics agree that our collection of Catullus was not
published by him, but by some too zealous friend

who after his death rescued all the scraps found among his papers, dicenda tacenda.

Before the second letter was composed however some time had elapsed, perhaps several months. Clodia had apparently offered some plausible explanation of the ugly rumors or had made promises of fidelity; at any rate Catullus was now able to refer to the matter with less show of impatience. Manlius had also recovered from his loneliness—was in fact happily betrothed, it seems. The body of the letter is a strange artificial composition in the mechanical Alexandrian manner built like a step-pyramid, ascending in uneven blocks of themes to a culminating point, and then descending in corresponding blocks to a conclusion. The verse groups are arranged in this fashion:

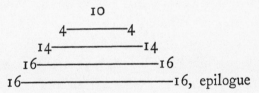

There is much prose in the poem, and much padding in order to attain the desired correspondences. The theme is strangely enough the kindness which Manlius had shown Catullus on the day to which he repeatedly refers. Let us hasten to say that a poem on so delicate a subject was never intended for gen-

eral reading. Even the names are obscured. The
word Lesbia is not mentioned. Manlius (pro-
nounced Mallius in daily speech) becomes Allius,
though at the first occurrence of the name it is preceded by *me* with elided vowel which would thus
reveal the poet's intention to the initiate. Even the
name of the man who first introduced Manlius to
Catullus is hidden under the term Afer (Munro's
emendation for the unreadable *aufert* in line 117).
I assume that Caelius, who had recently returned
from his African estates, is meant. The theme is of
course one which only Manlius could have understood. That Catullus should have cared to try metrical gymnastics in writing on that theme betrays a
morbid mood in one usually so wholesomely un-
self-conscious. It reveals too the grip of an over-
powering memory that was threatening to become an
obsession. We may be sure that his attempts to slur
over any suggestion of Clodia's faithlessness came
with an effort. His later epigrams written when his
mind had finally escaped from its first stupor show
that he had not even then regained complete self-
mastery.

The epistle is of some interest to the critic who
wishes to study the poet's struggles with the artificial
Greek forms that he had set out to learn. The subject matter needs a psychopath rather than a literary

critic for its successful interpretation. To those who desire an English version the Loeb translation, by Cornish, is perhaps the most reliable. I shall only add a suggestion as to some of the riddles of the poem. We have already said that 68 b is an independent poem, that the Afer (line 117), who first opened the way to Catullus' reconciliation with Clodia, seems to have been Caelius, and that the place of meeting was Manlius' palace. The domina of the palace (l. 28 and 116) was apparently some one who had charge of the bachelor household of Manlius, while *tua vita* (l. 115) may be his betrothed, the Junia Aurunculeia of poem 61. The division into corresponding blocks of verses necessitates placing a full stop after line 16. The picture of the waterfall must be read with what follows. It is one of the most striking landscapes in Latin verse and may be a reminiscence of one of the many capricious cascades high on the mountain side that one passes in the Adige valley as one travels north from Verona to Trent.

Qualis in aerii perlucens vertice montis
    Rivus muscoso prosilit e lapide,
Qui cum de prona praeceps est valle volutus,
    Per medium sensim transit iter populi.

Had Catullus written fifty years later, after the mountain folk had been pacified so that the Alps were made accessible to Roman travellers, he might well have discovered mountain landscape as a theme for poetry. I doubt very much whether Catullus sent this poem to Manlius. His use of cryptonyms shows that at the time of its composition he had some idea that it might in time be published, but I cannot conceive of his ever giving it circulation after he regained his mental balance.

What had occurred to Clodia during Catullus' absence we do not know. If, as it seems, we are concerned with the early stormy months of the year 59, this was indeed a period of rapidly changing conditions for her. Metellus died in February or March, Clodius was battling for leadership and his sister was "blowing the trumpet," [15] as Cicero puts it. Caelius, though opposed by the best lawyers of Rome, was then winning distinction by his daring and successful prosecution of Antonius. Meanwhile Catullus is reproaching Clodia with having broken the definite pledge of marriage she had given him. He had of course quite lost his sense of realities: Clodia's age, position, and exciting experiences in the hurly-burly of politics. The young poet had no position, no career in view that could fill the mind and occupy the energy of such a woman. It is not unlikely that after the meeting at Manlius' house she had again refused to meet him. It seems clear that what meant all of life to him was to her merely a temporary passion.

Three years after Metellus' death, when Clodia was in disgrace, the rumor was bandied about by her enemies that she had actually poisoned her husband.[16] Cicero then repeated the rumor in court, for he was as ready as any prosecuting attorney to-day to employ innuendo when it suited his purpose. Yet his rehearsal of his last conversations with Metellus in which they had discussed the activities of Clodius shows clearly enough that it was not a poisoned man with whom he had been talking in those days. Furthermore Metellus had just before his death been preparing to depart for a long campaign in Gaul, and would hardly have been an obstacle to Clodia's enjoyment of the pleasures of Rome. The charge would not deserve even a passing reference were it not that commentators continue to repeat it as though it might possibly be true. The rumor apparently grew up later and may be considered a hostile comment upon Clodia's reckless life after she had definitely parted from Catullus. It is in fact not probable that many were aware of the rôle that she had played in the young poet's life until the full edition of his poems came out after his death, and then she too seems to have left the scene.

The case of Caelius, who had become her neighbor

on the Palatine, was quite different. He was a tall, fair, attractive man,[17] clever, not too scrupulous, an heir to a fortune though his allowance was somewhat limited. He was ambitious to make a mark in politics—and he was more nearly Clodia's age. Cicero is rather amusing when for designs of his own he spins a kind of Joseph and Potiphar tale, insisting that Caelius was shy and wished only to be let alone, that he was working hard and wanted to devote himself to his chosen career, but that Clodia had fallen in love with him and would listen to no refusals. Without taking Cicero's remarks too seriously, one can nevertheless comprehend the attraction for her of a handsome young man who seemed to require the expenditure of a certain amount of effort.

Catullus found on his return to Rome—we are still probably in the year 59—that Clodia did not wish to see him. He knew now that she loved Caelius, his former friend. There are a number of brief poems and epigrams that belong to this period. He pleads and chides in turn, reminds her of her promises, reviles her for her faithlessness. It all seems aimless and of course proves futile. In the seventieth Catullus reminds Clodia rather bitterly of an old promise:

She said she would be my wife even if Jove should woo her. She said, but what a woman says

to her ardent lover should be written in wind or
running water.

Presently he repeats the reminder and adds a new
avowal (72):

> You said then that Catullus was more than Jove
> to you. I loved you not as one loves a mistress,
> but with the love of parents and children. Now I
> know you, a creature of less worth, yet my love has
> grown more passionate.

His mood changes from day to day and he does not
always comprehend what it is that he actually feels:
hate and love and suffering confuse him (85):

> Odi et amo, quare id faciam, fortasse requiris.
> Nescio, sed fieri sentio et excrucior.

There seems to have been a temporary reconciliation,
though it probably lasted for only a short time, and
Catullus felt no great assurance of its actuality
(109):

> Sweet is the love you offer with the pledge that
> it will endure. Heaven attend the pledge. May
> her promise be sincere that we may live in love all
> our days.

But there is at least for a while an end of torture for
him.

We do not know what part Catullus played in the
stormy politics of this year which involved his friend

Calvus. In the autumn the young men who had lampooned the triumvirs were openly accused of taking part in a conspiracy to murder them. Curio, who had done much reckless talking, quickly cleared himself. Several other discontented republicans, especially "a band of young men led by Curio," were named by Vettius,[18] who pretended to turn "state's evidence." Curio's band of young men had been the group that two years before had aided Clodia. Now allegiances had shifted, but the group that wrote the lampoons against the triumvirs contained many of the young rebels active in the Clodian trial. There is a mysterious epigram in Catullus (98) which may possibly refer to this Vettius though the manuscripts favor the rare name Vittius or Victius.

Vittius, the old proverb on the prattler was made
   for you,
If you mean to ruin all of us you have but to open
   your mouth.

If these lines are indeed addressed to Vettius it is likely that some of the Caesarian lampoons of which we shall speak later should also be referred to this period.

There are two wedding songs in the Catullian collection, one in hexameters, apparently an exercise in form (62), the other (61) a very finished poem of

nearly 240 glyconic lines (some of which are lost).
The hexameter poem is strangely constructed in
amoebaean form for antiphonal choruses of boys and
girls. The first four stanzas are spoken by the re-
spective chorus leaders, giving "stage directions," as
it were, to their troupes; then as the evening star
arises and the procession enters, the choruses sing,
the boys greeting the wedding star with joy, the
maidens in decorously feigned sorrow. In form this
of course resembles the amoebaean contest-songs of
Theocritus, and it is more than surprising to find it
employed for the purposes of a wedding. The suggestion has been made that it might be a translation
of a song of Sappho, but form and contents both
preclude this possibility. It may be that Catullus was
casting about for some novel form that would suit the
circumstances of a Roman wedding where singing
had not been customary, and that, finding the first
attempt unsatisfactory, he tried a new staging in the
sixty-first. At any rate the form gives a tone of
unreality to the earlier one. Nevertheless it has
some very appealing passages, as for instance the
lines of the maidens' chorus beginning:

Ut flos in saeptis secretus nascitur hortis.

The longer wedding song (61) was certainly
written for a definite occasion. It will be remem-

bered that in Catullus' letter to Manlius (68 b) there
was a reference to one who was apparently his betrothed (the *tua vita* is not identified with *domina*).
It is only reasonable to assign the wedding song
written for Manlius to a period not very remote
from that, and the exuberance of the song gives
evidence of a time of relative tranquillity in the
poet's life. The wedding was no ordinary affair.
Manlius Torquatus was a direct descendant of a
famous hero of the fourth century, and his father
had been consul in 66. He himself later earned
the rare distinction among literary men of being
represented as one of the scholarly interlocutors in
Cicero's *De Finibus*. The bride was an Aurunculeia
by birth, and a relative of Brutus by adoption; and
the Aurunculeius Cotta, who met disaster as Caesar's
legate in Gaul in 54 may well have been her brother.
Catullus' *Epithalamium* was probably not written to
be sung at the wedding itself—the Roman wedding
ordinarily had no place for a song during the rites.
It was rather the poet's wedding gift, intended to be
one of the family treasures. The suggestion for it
doubtless came to Catullus from his reading of
Sappho, but we must not suppose that we have here
her actual words translated into Latin. The very
progression of the song proves that the scene is
Roman, not Greek. Catullus chooses for his setting

the moment after the sacred rite before the altar
has been completed, and the groom has departed to
open the door of the new home to receive the bride
at her coming. The song begins before the bride
steps out to lead the procession, it accompanies her
with good wishes not without some orthodox lines
for the groom in the spirit of a boisterous Roman
charivari. The song continues until in Roman fashion the bride is lifted over the threshold of her new
home and the doors are closed. The meter is one
of his happiest, a glyconic rhythm frequently used
by Sappho. The short lines have a good trochaic
march-beat, with a quickening dactyl in the middle,
and an effective pause at the end of every fifth line.
The poet's spontaneity, his rush of mellow sound,
his liquid naturalness, his opulence of color, his
exuberance of spirit here fill all the senses. The
poet is inviting all the world to marry. The song
gives abundant proof that he could sing another's
happiness as well as his own. It was the Torquatus
stanza doubtless that Tennyson had in mind when he
called him "tenderest of Roman poets":

> Torquatus volo parvulus
>   Matris e gremio suae
>   Porrigens teneras manus
> Dulce rideat ad patrem
>   Semihiante labello.

The mood of that song was not to last long. Lesbia did not love him, and his fears that her "everlasting pledge" might be written in sand gave way to certainty and to jealousy. Not only is Caelius accused of treachery to him but others as well—who may have been mere screens to hide her real intentions. It would be hazardous to attempt to interpret Clodia's behavior at this time since we have no word from her. *Miser Catulle, desinas ineptire* (8) is perhaps the most poignant of Catullus' poems written during this period, and one of the most naïve utterances of love in all the range of poetry. We can comprehend his determination not to hope, and his inevitable harking back to the day:

> Cum ventitabas quo puella ducebat,
> Amata nobis quantum amabitur nulla,

his insistence upon self-mastery in staccato phrases that betray his helplessness:

> Sed obstinata mente perfer, obdura.
> Vale, puella. Iam Catullus obdurat.

But at that moment he catches at the most hopeless pretext to plead again, the fancy that she too must somehow feel the same pain:

> At tu dolebis, cum rogaberis nulla.
> Scelesta, vae te! quae tibi manet vita!

It would be a complete misunderstanding of his mood to attribute such lines to vanity. What possesses him is an imaginative sympathy born of the intensity of a memory that identifies his mistress with himself and that makes a severance in their emotions seem impossible. No one else during these many centuries has so simply betrayed his primary impulses. We have grown too sophisticated for such poetry. And scholars, writing commentaries on these lines for callow freshmen, soberly remark in the face of all standard usage that *scelesta vae te* is satire!

Another poem belonging to this period is the well-known prayer-song (76)—the first example of a Roman love-elegy that we have—and the best. But the name of the type hardly matters; that was invented long after Catullus was dead. Here again the poet is trying with what resolution he can command to forget his love though he cannot say whether it will mean life or death to him. He has no sense of guilt—he has served love in utter fidelity. That at least heaven must respect. Is not such piety enough?

Non iam illud quaero contra ut me diligat illa,
aut quod non potis est, esse pudica velit;
ipse valere opto et taetrum hunc deponere morbum.
O di reddite mi hoc pro pietate mea.

Even his pagan gods must have been nonplussed at such a prayer. And if Clodia concluded that Caelius was a less puzzling and more comfortable companion for her leisure hours than her young poet, her conclusion would hardly be incomprehensible.

To the student of literature there is an interesting revelation in these epigrams and elegies of how new literary types were apt to take shape, in this instance of how genius, using conventional forms to new ends, begets new forms. Catullus never strove for novelty. In that he was like the Greeks, who whether in architecture, in literature, or in sculpture, tried only to express themselves as nearly adequately and perfectly as might be in the generally accepted forms. A more striking originality no people has ever revealed and yet with no conscious respect for novelty or originality as such. We can trace the standard ornaments of the Doric entablature from wood to marble through hundreds of years, we can see how old ornaments, necessitated by the use of one material, were conventionally kept in succeeding materials where they had no *raison d'être* except that of convention. Progress revealed itself in more carefully elaborated proportions, in more perfect adaptation to new needs and in more exquisite design and workmanship; never in striving after mere originality of design.

The Greek epigram begins in the style of epitaphs upon tombstones. The space is limited, what is to be said must be said tersely and effectively. The theme is stated, commented upon and neatly concluded. For such themes the elegiac couplet lent itself well: the even-flowing hexameter line for theme, the broken hexameter for slower reiteration. The form came to be used in brief literary compositions, in fixing a momentary thought, conveying a fleeting sentiment, in dedicating or presenting a book, in pithy comments on life's vanities and the ways of death, on fate's fickleness, or in sketching a picture: a garden scene, the beauty of a rose, or a statue of Praxiteles. Some of the poets of the Greek anthology, writing in a period of changing social fashions, came very near using it for love-poetry, but no one of them ever stepped wholly outside of the conventional conceits. Pretty epigrams on Cupid's wings, the first kiss, the love that turns to hate, unrequited love, inconstancy—all these they wrote, but impersonally, and in daintily balanced phrases. Venus and Cupid never quite emerge from the marble form. Catullus of course had read many of the Greek epigrams. He had the average reader's unanalyzed impression of what the conventional form should be. When he wrote his *Odi et amo* he was, without serious concern as to form, naturally writing in a stand-

ard couplet: he states his paradox and points it with
a line that leaves it all the more a paradox. What
we see at once is, however, that it is he, Catullus,
who has felt the words that are written, and even if
we did not know the story of Lesbia we should know
that there must be a woman of flesh and blood behind those words.

A poem to which we have already referred (70) is
a similar epigram so far as its external form is concerned:

> She said—
> But what a woman says—

Catullus returns to the same theme in 72, arranged
again in paradox-answer design. The first two and
the last two lines have the same query and reply, but
the four central lines are packed with the poet's tor-
turing memory:

> 1-2 Dicebas—
> 3-6 Dilexi tum—
> 7-8 Qui potis est?

The Greek epigram is here obviously changing into
a lyric under our eyes.[19] And in the prayer (76),
referred to above, it is a full-fledged lyric of twenty-
six lines which has even abandoned the standard
epigrammatic form. There is nothing left but the
woe of his own broken love.

Cornelius Gallus, a few years after Catullus' death, seems to have understood what had happened to the old Greek form, and to have adopted the free elegiac form of Catullus here and there for the expression of his love for his equally inconstant Cytheris; and Propertius and Ovid, while acknowledging Mimnermus and Callimachus as their masters in the elegiac narrative, credited Gallus with the suggestion of the specific form. Catullus was of course, though unconsciously, the originator.

IV

THE CIRCLE OF CATULLUS

THE year 58 was as exciting politically as the preceding year. Clodius had finally reached his tribuneship by a turn of fortune which now seems somewhat
ludicrous. Caesar had at first opposed his ambitions,
for Clodius might at any moment get beyond control.
But one day Cicero had made bold to criticize the
triumvirs. Caesar decided that such criticism must
stop and that it could most effectively be checked
by giving Cicero's bitterest enemy some power of
action. Caesar accordingly subscribed to the conversion of Clodius into a plebeian and aided him in
the election to the tribunate. Clodius at once an-
nounced that it was his intention to propose the
banishment of Cicero on the charge that the execution of the Catilinarian conspirators had been illegal.
Caesar was now long overdue in his province, for
the Helvetians were loading their luggage for an
invasion of Gaul. But Caesar with long years of
work ahead of him had no intention of leaving until
he had Rome properly in control. He allowed
Clodius to get rid of Cato by sending him on a dis-

agreeable diplomatic mission to Cyprus. He hoped that Clodius' threats would drive Cicero into giving pledges of good behavior. The pledges did not come. Cicero was willing to plead with his friends for their intervention and help, but he would not promise abject compliance. He pleaded with Pompey and the consuls, and he even asked Atticus to go and confer with Clodia! Caesar still waited—news came that the Helvetians were crossing the Rhine. Now he could delay no longer. So he gave Clodius free reign. The plebeians at the instigation of Clodius and with the secret approval of Caesar passed the bill to exile Cicero. That day Caesar rode off toward Geneva, covering a distance of 700 miles on horseback in a week. Then began the campaign that ended ten years later with the conquest of Gaul and the Civil War. At Rome, with real leadership gone in the absence of Caesar and Cicero, political intrigues broke out everywhere. Clodius passed a number of reckless party measures against the advice of Pompey, and Caesar made no effort to hinder them since he did not greatly care if Pompey's reputation should gradually be frittered away in futile opposition. Clodius was at least grateful enough to Caesar not to carry his independence to the point of breaking with that powerful man. The young epigrammatists now amused themselves mostly by shooting occasional arrows at the bulky and helpless Pompey. Calvus went somewhat farther, throwing down the gauntlet to the whole triumvirate by prosecuting Caesar's most faithful tool, the ex-tribune Vatinius. It was a daring attack for a youth not yet twenty-four years of age. His speech made a great impression at the time and was still read a hundred years later as a model of studied art in seemingly artless form. Quintilian in referring to it remarks that Vatinius cried out: "Must I then be convicted because the prosecutor is so eloquent?" Catullus refers to the speech in one of his lighter epigrams (no. 53):

> Risi nescio quem modo e corona,
> qui, cum mirifice Vatiniana
> meus crimina Calvus explicasset,
> admirans ait haec manusque tollens:
> "di magni, salaputium disertum!"

Vatinius had too strong a backing to be overturned by Calvus, but his hatred of his prosecutor seems to have become a proverb. Catullus refers to it in an amusing letter of thanks (14) he sent Calvus for a Saturnalia present he had received. Calvus had waggishly sent him an anthology of particularly bad poetry—apparently had it selected and copied for him. Catullus protests: "If I did not love you, my sweet friend, I should hate you as Vatinius for your gift. Did you get that volume from some impecunious client as fee for your labor? On the Saturnalia too when one should be happy! But I'll requite it. To-morrow I shall go to the book shop and buy you complete sets of Caesius, Aquinus and Suffenus."

The passage is interesting if only as a proof that the town was full of poetasters. Caesius and Aquinus are but names. Suffenus [20] seems to be a nickname for Alfenus Varus, who later became a distinguished jurist, many of whose legal opinions have survived in Justinian's great code. Alfenus in fact came from the Po region at about the time Catullus did, and he too was combining verse-writing, politics and law. He seems to have had property in land and shops at home, and as a parvenu he was the butt of jokes at Rome because of his social ambitions. Yet he had done Catullus some favor once, and the young poet, always too trustful, gave him his confidence—presumably regarding Lesbia—which he forthwith betrayed. The thirtieth, *Alfene immemor atque unanimis false sodalibus,* is a pitiful poem chiding him for his thoughtlessness. The poem seems to belong to the year 59. The two men were of course no longer friends after that, and in *Suffenus iste, Vare, quem probe nosti* (22), Catullus has some sharp things to say of the boorish poetry

of the man. The poem is addressed to the young
critic Quintilius Varus, and *iste* is meant to suggest
"that young man who bears your name, Varus," or
"the young man from your native town."

> Your friend is, to be sure, charming and a good
> talker. He also writes volumes of verses and has
> them all issued in de luxe editions; but when you
> open the books to read you find at once that he is
> still the boorish farmer that he used to be. But
> he enjoys his verse and admires it. "O wad some
> power the giftie gie us!"

Horace who twenty years later knew the fellow in
the days of his success made a similar remark which
was meant to suggest this epigram of Catullus.

The Quintilius Varus to whom that poem was addressed and a humorous one later (10)—*Varus me
meus ad suos amores*—was to be a critic of some importance, and it is as well to take his measure now.
He too was a well-to-do provincial, from the colony
of Cremona, and therefore a fellow countryman.
The Po-valley was a rich new country and was now
sending a stream of happily endowed young fellows
to Rome for initiation into the studies that might
lead to an honorable political career. We have already mentioned Catullus, Cinna, and Alfenus, here
is Varus, and Gallus and Vergil were soon to come
—and there were others who may be omitted for

the present. They all show a keen interest in literature, and most of them make their name in writing rather than in politics. Caesar's control of the political position had something to do with turning them away from a public career. Varus did not progress far in public life. Some twelve years later we find him at Naples studying philosophy with Vergil, in the Epicurean school of Philodemus. Vergil, in speaking of their school-days together, addresses the sixth eclogue to him.[21] At his death in 24 B.C. Horace sent an ode of consolation to Vergil, and in his *Ars Poetica* speaks of him as a candid critic of the most exacting ideals. Varus, therefore, was an important link between the late republic and the early Augustan times. Taking our clue from Horace we shall not be far wrong in considering him one of those who formed their style after the pregnant and lucid work of Catullus and passed on to the next generation what they had learned. In that case it is worth noting that it is to Varus that Catullus indicates the crudities and verbosity of Alfenus' style. Catullus is here the teacher in formulating the lesson that Horace later emphasizes in speaking of Lucilius, even though Horace, disliking the later Alexandrian style of Catullus, did not care to acknowledge him as his master.

There is in fact a close connection between Catul-

lus' style in his early verses and the "plain" style
of Calvus' Atticism though it is more a connection
of taste than of theory. Catullus' "plainness" is due
partly to his lack of pretensions. He does not yet
consider himself a literary man. He is still merely
writing for himself and his friends. And the vocabulary of prose accomplishes so fully what he
wishes that he finds no need of the adornment that
the critics talked so much about. Would that he
might have written thus without ambition, without
sophistication, without elaborate models and poetic
theory for a long lifetime! If he had, the history of
Roman poetry would have been different. Calvus,
as we have said, attained to some of the same effects
in prose by conscious choice and by revolting from
the senatorial prose style toward the model of Lysias.
Doubtless the two men discussed their work, their
preferences and their theories. They might have
issued an interesting essay not unlike the famous
Preface of Wordsworth and Coleridge. As we have
said, there were youngsters like Varus and Pollio who
imbibed much good sense from Calvus and Catullus
and gave it to the next generation. Horace certainly
profited, even if indirectly. But since Horace lacked
the natural gift of translucent and inevitable directness, he had to attain these qualities by diligent

labor, and his effects therefore never seem as spontaneous as Catullus'.

The year 58 was not a pleasant one for Catullus. Not only did he direct several bitter epigrams against Caelius but against others as well, notably an unknown Egnatius, who may have been the epic poet of that name. By implication they all make ugly charges against Clodia. She, in fact, had received much wealth from her husband's estate, and was now spending no little time at the seaside, especially at Baiae. Between times she was keeping open house on the Palatine, giving elaborate parties in her private park near the Tiber where she provided banquets and water sports for the very gay set. Catullus was not invited.

At the end of the year, however, the poet found wholesome distraction. Memmius, though an opponent of Caesar—he had in fact tried to impeach him after his consulship—had secured the praetorship in 58 and was allotted the province of Bithynia in Asia Minor for 57. Being a poetaster himself and a patron of poets—this is the Memmius of the Lucretian dedication—he took Catullus and Cinna on his staff. Ordinarily young men accepted such positions in order to acquire some experience and knowledge in what we might call "colonial affairs," and it was assumed that they were preparing for a political career, the normal career of young men of family and leisure. It is not impossible that Catullus thought he had wasted time enough, and, tired of the *otium* which he had cursed years before, was now ready to enter public life. However, a governor was permitted to take friends merely for the sake of companionship or to serve as a staff of private advisers. Catullus had peculiar reasons for going; he desired to get away from scenes of sorrow, and he doubtless wished to visit the tomb of his brother at Troy. There was no regular salary attached to this office, but it was understood that the governor would pay the travelling and living expenses of his staff, that he might award them gifts from booty if there were any, and also give them some funds from the appropriated allowance if this were not all used in necessary expenses. If we are to believe Catullus, Memmius gave nothing.

The band probably did not set out till early in the spring of 57. It was as well not to reach Brundisium at least till the spring sailing began in March. The journey led through the town of Venusia where Horace lived, then a boy of seven years, to Brundisium, past Corfu, through the gulf of Corinth to Athens, then by sea up into the Bosporus to Bithynia, opposite Byzantium. Arrival would probably be about April, and Memmius' year in the province

would last till his successor arrived the following
spring. In point of fact Catullus departed for home
in the spring of 56 soon after the first spring winds
came—that is, in March or April. We actually have
more definite references to his joy in the departure
after the year is over, the homeward journey, and
his longed-for home-coming (46, 31, 4) than to any
experiences during his year abroad. That he wrote
some verse during the months of semi-leisure is not
unlikely. We happen to hear that Cinna [22] in any
case embodied his experiences in a "steamer-letter"
to Pollio who was then about to sail eastward.
Catullus' epitaph to his brother may well have been
inspired by a visit to his grave. We have spoken of it
above. It is also usually agreed that his own experiences on the broad sea, sailing the course into the
Bosporus that was taken by the Argonauts, may have
suggested his brief epic (64). The style of the poem
seems to fall into two periods, so that a part of it
may well have been done in Bithynia. We shall
recur to it later.

The *Attis* [23] also (63), which is probably his most
striking composition, might well have been inspired
by what he saw of the Cybele worship and the Troad
on this expedition, though of that there is no definite
proof. This poem is exceedingly dramatic and per-
vaded by feelings that Catullus—unhappy as he was

in Bithynia—found easy to imagine in that far-off country. A young man is represented as converted in religious frenzy to the worship of Magna Mater. To become an acolyte of the goddess he sails to Mt. Ida in the Troad where Cybele lives in her temple, goes through the awful initiation which requires emasculation, and leads his companions in the riotous worship of the Great Mother. After a night's rest he awakens to the full realization of what he has done. Standing on the seashore he looks back over the water in vain longing for his home, his country, his friends—knowing the while that he can never return to that life again. Cybele sees him and sends her lions to drive him back to his devotions.

The theme had been used before in some unknown manner by Callimachus. But this poem of Catullus is not a translation or a paraphrase—though it may contain suggestions from a previous poem. Nothing that we have of Callimachus justifies the supposition that he could have written with the keen penetration, the sympathy, the fire and dash of this poem. Whether, however, the suggestion came from his reading or from observation matters little. Catullus himself in visiting Lesbia on the Palatine had had occasion enough to learn about the rites of this weird cult, for only a few yards to the rear of her house the beating of the timbrels to the wild Galliambic rhythm could be heard. Rome had nearly two centuries before imported the cult, and it was a Claudia, a famous vestal virgin from among Clodia's forbears, who had been instrumental in bringing the barge with the mother-goddess up the Tiber. Even Cicero in his famous tirade against Clodia compares the two women, and Catullus could not have escaped some reference to the story.

That the rhythm of this song was understood at Rome is evident from Varro, who in satirizing what he called religious insanity, points his readers to the Cybele temple on the Palatine, and while referring to it shifts his verse into the Galliambic rhythm. To be sure the staid Romans who insisted on dignity and beauty in worship had long ago built an enclosure about the strange cult and had forbidden Romans to become initiates. But once a year, in April, in order to avoid sacrilege, they let the rites go on openly. Not till a century later when a Claudius was on the throne at Rome was the cult accepted with full approval. Catullus, therefore, had good reason to know something about it, and he had heard the dance and wild singing before he went east. However, his choice of the shrine on Mt. Ida in the Troad as the scene of his poem would seem to indicate that the vital suggestion for it came on the very spot. And doubtless the thought of what exile in that dreary land would have meant to him, enabled him to visualize the plight of Attis with such utter poignancy. The setting is Greek, and the hero is represented as a Greek, for in view of the legal prohibition at Rome, a Roman priest would hardly be plausible. But the deep home longing, the desire for fellowship in one's country and city, the dread of religious frenzy are wholly Roman.

The meter—as already noticed—is that rapid, orgiastic, dance-march rhythm that Catullus had heard more than once. The most normal lines run:

But there are many substitutions and resolutions and here and there also silent half feet. The use of a seven foot line probably means a silent foot at the end also, and the tribrach in the sixth foot produces a clash between word accent and verse ictus which gives an effect of lawlessness. The effect is heightened by the use of long words at the end of lines so that the clash must come in adjacent feet of the same word. The verse must be read with the tambourine in mind, for the beat of the instrument produces syncopation at the point of clashing, while the feet move on in a regular dance rhythm.

Simul haec comitibus Attis cecinit notha mulier, thiasus repente linguis trepidantibus ululat,

leue tympanum remugit, caua cymbala recrepant,
uiridem citus adit Idam properante pede chorus.
Furibunda simul anhelans uaga uadit animam agens
comitata tympano Attis per opaca nemora dux,
ueluti iuuenca uitans onus indomita iugi:
rapidae ducem secuntur Gallae properipedem;
itaque, ut domum Cybelles tetigere lassulae.

The experiment in Tennyson's Boadicea quite fails
to reproduce the quality of the meter since the conflict between stress and quantity, so important in
Galliambics, cannot be effectively played with in
English verse.

Our scholarly metrists, who must have an orderly
explanation for all meters, showing just how every
one developed out of the hypothetical Indo-Euro-
pean forms, accept Hephaestion's pedantic explanation that this is in origin an Ionic meter $\smile \smile - -$
mathematically reshaped by Alexandrian poets. To
the younger generation who have had to learn several
new rhythms in recent dances, these old theories
read like a parody on Casaubon. It is true, strange
though it may seem, that Alexandrian poetasters did
deliberately shape new meters by addition and sub-
traction of shorts and longs in various parts of the
line.[24] But no vital meter ever sprang up in such
mechanical fashion. Rhythms that have survived
have corresponded to the beat or wail of instruments

that kept time to leaping, dancing or marching feet. Feet in their movements are fairly well restricted to regular intervals of time, but the timbrels, especially by the use of syncopation, can set the arms and head off on a secondary rhythm which clashes with the tread of the feet, or can transfer the beat with more or less regularity from the tread to the lift of the foot. And such effects even to-day are more frequently sought after in Arabic, Berber and Turkish music than in European forms. The syncopated time which has been so popular in recent dance music is of course not an adaptation of classical rhythms. It is an importation from the jungle. The very fact that Varro when on the Palatine heard the Anatolian priests of Cybele, imported to perform these rites in their native manner, chant and dance in this rhythm is proof enough that it was neither Greek nor an artificial invention. Catullus got it from the same source as Callimachus did. He had known it both from the performances of the "Galli" on the Palatine, and from the dances of the priests of the Asiatic temples.

For the return journey Catullus bought a "Nicaean bark" and Cinna procured eight good Cappadocian slaves whom he could use as litter carriers at home. They could of course also serve as oarsmen and workmen on the yacht. Catullus who was brought up on Lake Garda could assume the rôle of skipper. So the two poets bade a happy farewell to the chilly blasts that roared down Nicaea's valleys from the giant snow-capped Olympus, and a tender good-bye to the companions of the winter (46, 10, 4). They spent the summer cruising among the famous islands of the Aegean, coasting down as far as Rhodes before striking across past the Cyclades to Athens. By mere chance we have a brief epigram that Cinna sent to a friend with a presentation copy of Aratus which he had picked up at some Bithynian book-stall. It was a curious copy written on mallow leaves, he says, and carried home all the way from Prusa on his friend's yacht. Over the isthmus of Corinth it would be necessary to have the yacht drawn on the railway that was much used for the portage of light craft. Thence they sailed through the Gulf of Corinth, the Adriatic and on up the river Po. It is questionable whether a sea-going yacht could at that time be towed up the Mincio past Mantua all the way to Garda. It would hardly be possible to-day. But at any rate the portage distance on a stout pair of trucks would not be far.

Catullus' greeting to Sirmio is full of the old hearty boyish laughter. The sea had been kind to him.

Salve, o venusta Sirmio atque ero gaude,
gaudete vosque, O Lydiae lacus undae,
ridete quidquid est domi cachinnorum.

A year later when he regrets that his yacht, which he
had brought home with so much labor, must lie
unused he entrusts it to the protection of Castor and
Pollux in a poem of perfect iambics, written to remind himself of that long and happy cruise. It is
the only Latin poem which attained the distinction of
a parody that has survived, and that was written by
his all-but-neighbor, Vergil. The Mantuan may
have had especial cause to remember the poem for
the yacht must have passed through and halted at
Mantua on its passage home: Vergil was then a boy
of nearly fourteen.

When Catullus reached Rome he found many
changes. Caelius who had wasted most of two years
in the gay life of Clodia's entourage at Rome and
Baiae, and had even at her bidding permitted himself to become an instrument in the rough political
thuggery of Clodius, had finally come to his senses
during Catullus' absence, and had entered the active
life of the Forum again. In doing so he had somehow incurred the vengeful anger of Clodia, who had
determined to punish him. The involved story
comes out only in fragments in Cicero's defence of
Caelius, delivered in the spring of 56, but it runs

something like this.[25] Ptolemy the king of Egypt, driven out of his kingdom by his people in 57, had taken refuge in Rome. Since the triumvirs held the Egyptian bonds, they had pledged him their support. His restoration, however, was delayed because a division of opinion arose as to how it should be accomplished. Pompey desired the assignment, while Caesar wished to keep Pompey off the stage in obscurity. Meanwhile a large delegation arrived from Alexandria to oppose the king's restoration. Clodius apparently had orders from Caesar to keep this delegation at a distance so that it would not drive the senate into hasty compliance with Pompey's wishes. The delegation accordingly was kept occupied at Naples, and Caelius seems to have been employed by Clodia in the amusing task of helping to terrorize them. There were riots both at Naples and Puteoli and in one of these the leader of the delegation was actually killed. Calvus attempted to secure an indictment against one of the Clodian group, but failed. Then came a reshifting of the scene. Caelius, disgusted with his stupid rôle, broke away from Clodia, while Caesar renewed his friendship with Pompey, dropping his fantastic instrument, Clodius. When Caelius was now haled to court because of his part in the rioting, Clodia—bent on personal revenge—placed incriminating information at

the service of the prosecution.   Caelius begged his
old master, Cicero, who had now been recalled from
exile, to undertake his defence, promised to be a
model young conservative in the future, and revealed
the fact that Clodia was supporting the attack.
Cicero accepted the case.   The prosecution made the
mistake of bringing in character witnesses to expose
Caelius' riotous life at Baiae, and Clodia was so
blinded by a desire for revenge that in revealing details she exposed herself.   Cicero in his defence of
Caelius took advantage of this revelation and threw
all the onus of Caelius' misdeeds on Clodia.   The
speech seethes with innuendo.   There are but few
direct charges, and the reader who is acquainted with
Cicero's amazing command of psychological devices
soon observes that the old lawyer is careful in every
sentence to avoid prosecution for libel.   The speech
is full of contingent and concessive clauses that
would protect him in case of cross examination.   But
Cicero had saved up two years of hatred against
Clodius and his sister; and he now gave vent to it.
There are pages of suggestions and hints, of generalized tirades against women who break normal
conventions, of unforgettable phrases that are not
always pertinent to the case.   He ranges in his attack from solemn abjuration, through biting sarcasm
to apt citations from the comic poets.

Caelius was acquitted, and Clodia lost the last shred of her reputation in Roman society. Of course no proof was offered that she deserved all the titles that were then invented by Caelius and Cicero. The worst charge came from Caelius himself who called her Clytemnestra, which hinted at the murder of her husband, and *quadrantaria*—the penny-slut. In fact Clodia had hidden her liaisons with no little care, and Caelius' own salacious phrase "Coa (coeo) in triclinio, Nola (nolo) in cubiculo," would naturally indicate a woman who was more guilty of conscience-less coquetry than of actual vice. However, there was enough misbehavior to shock Roman society, and when it was exposed in the glare of the most brilliant oratory of Cicero and Caelius, the world believed the worst, and even Catullus seems to have accepted the blackest innuendo as actual fact (no. 11). In any case Clodia never again regained a position of influence.

All this took place while Catullus was in the East. On his return he seems to have lived at Rome for a while, probably working fitfully upon his *Peleus and Thetis*. He kept up some social connections. We have, for instance, a punning epigram on the style of the pompously ornate and humorless Sestius, a friend of Pompey. Sestius had delivered a speech in 56. When Catullus was invited to dine with him, he naturally thought it proper to read Sestius' speech in order to be prepared with a flattering theme for table talk.   The oration, however, was so "frigid" (the Latin term for ornate) that the poet "caught a cold" and had to retire to his villa at Tivoli to regain his health (44).   That happens to be his only reference to his possessing a country villa near Rome. The epigram is welcome as an indication of his agreement with Calvus in approving the "plain style" in Latin prose.

There are also some more or less personal lampoons on men less well known which seem to belong to this period: on Naso, somewhat too ubiquitous, on Cominius, who has fallen so desperately in love that his friends can never find him, on Piso, Caesar's father-in-law, who had given beggarly treatment to his staff in Macedonia while other members of the staff, like the thieving Socration, had fared better, on the impecunius Furius, who is always asking for a loan and never paying, and on the cockney Arrius. There are finally not a few scurrilous epigrams in the manner of the time which do not grace the haphazard collection.

Some of these men will come into the story again and it may be as well to speak of them here.   Catullus strikes at the proconsul Piso (47) for neglecting his good friends on the staff, Veranius and Fabullus, and enriching Porcius and Socration [26] who helped him in his "thieving." The year is 56, when Cicero in a public speech attacked Piso for robbing his province Macedonia of money and objects of art, and Cicero there says that Piso's boon companion is the Greek philosopher and poet, Philodemus. We have already noticed that Catullus used a poem of Philodemus some four years before this (no. 13) in writing an invitation to Fabullus. Now this Socration, "Pseudo-Socrates," can hardly be any one but Philodemus. Presumably one philosopher sufficed for his train. Since Piso brought back art objects, his Greek friend could be of service in giving hints as to what was worth buying (we need not necessarily believe Cicero's charge that the statuary was stolen—a proconsul's buying in his province was at best not beyond cavil). The famous Herculanean villa where Philodemus' manuscripts were found seems quite certainly to have been Piso's. It contained the kind of bronzes that Piso would have found in Macedonia and Byzantium. Philodemus later set up a school of Epicurean philosophy where Vergil met him, and we shall find presently that he exerted some little influence over Horace. There are over thirty epigrams of his in the Greek Anthology, in one of which Piso is mentioned. They are probably work of the period 65-55 B.C. Catul-

lus had certainly read them. They have something
of the precision and delicacy of finish of Catullus'
own poems and may have influenced Catullus in
more than the one effort mentioned above.

To Furius and a friend we find several lampoons
directed in Catullus' last years, some that did not
deserve preservation. They are the kind of thing
that he threw off in those verse-writing contests with
Calvus and in their frankness remind us of the
medieval "gabs." The sedulous editor of Catullus
apparently rescued all the poems that he found,
irrespective of their merits. Apropos of some criticism on the part of Furius that Catullus' verses to
Juventius (48) were effeminate he makes the interesting defence (16): "You shall have a trouncing
for your criticism. A poet must himself be clean,
but his verses need not be. Those lines were written
not for children but for the amusement of grey-
beards who demand spicy fare." [27]   Ovid and
Martial and even the staid Pliny repeat the statement later in excusing salacious verses. Whatever
we may think of a society which invites the formula-
tion of such an apology, the statement must be taken
at face value. Nevertheless it would seem from
the tone of these later epigrams that Catullus' associations with Memmius' cohort and the Greeks of

Bithynia in 57-6 brought a strain into his epigrams which lowered their poetic worth.

The Furius in question seems to be Furius Bibaculus whom we shall meet as an opponent of Horace, and we shall have occasion to speak more fully of him then. He was about the same age as Catullus and like Catullus a Cisalpine. He had a checkered career, and we find him now lampooning Caesar, now praising him. He was particularly devoted to the critic Valerius Cato, and later seems to have defended the "new poets" against the Augustans. In one epigram to him (23) Catullus abuses him for constantly begging from his friends, and in another (26) perpetrates a pun about his debts (Your house is exposed, not to a gust of wind, but what is worse, to a banker's draft). Furius Bibaculus passed the suggestion on to his friend Valerius Cato, though changing the pun (You can solve every riddle of philology, but when you face a mortgage you are insolvent). I repeat these atrocities only because they appear to add an item to the proposed identification of the Catullian Furius with the well-known Furius Bibaculus.

Among the other light epigrams we find one (84) on "Arrius" [28] who had acquired a "cockney" accent from his low-born grandmother, a pronunciation which bewrayed him distressingly. In Cicero's letters a year or two later we find a number of jokes of the same kind at the expense of Pompey's cousin, Hirrus, who was attempting to mount to high office by means of Pompey's favor. His pronunciation (dropping of the *h*, and lisping) made him the butt of so many jokes that progress was difficult. Since Catullus was at this time engaged in lampooning the triumvirs and their henchmen, it is quite likely that "Arrius" is a slight disguise for 'Irrus.

But Catullus did not confine himself to the underlings. Like Calvus, Memmius, Furius and others he shot his arrows straight at Caesar and Pompey. The severest attack was delivered over the head of Caesar's chief engineer, Mamurra, the man who probably built the famous bridge over the Rhine, planned the military roads, and designed the forts which Caesar describes with so much gusto in his commentaries. Mamurra was by all means the best military engineer of his day. He had had excellent training with Pompey in the Mithridatic war, then with Caesar in his proconsulship in Spain, and now had developed a transport and engineering machine which was operating perfectly in Gaul. Incidentally, we hear that he was the first to build a palace of marble at Rome, and when we remember that Carrara marble—from Caesar's province—was first used at this time, we may surmise that it was this engineer who set going the commerce in this marble which has since extended to all parts of the world. The fellow received a very handsome allowance from Caesar, and after his hard work in the sloughs of Gaul he liked during the winter to return with Caesar to the Cisalpine province to enjoy himself. He spent as easily as he made. His capacity to lavish money was equalled only by his vanity. One may imagine what a sensation he made in his holiday toga when he came to Verona to display himself. There are a few early jibes of Catullus at the love-making of this wastrel from Formiae with a Veronese cocotte. They are harmless enough. The later ones (written in the poet's last year, since the invasion of Britain is mentioned) are far more bitter. There can be little doubt that Mamurra's courting had now come closer to Catullus' own home. We need cite only one of these poisoned epigrams (29). It has to be read in Latin, a language that can be very direct. In these perfect iambic lines, composed from Rome's everyday words in phrases that seem the simplest prose, the steady, sure fall of the ax is as well-aimed as even Caesar's prose might make it, and the edge has a filed keenness that only Catullus' Latin knows.

Quis hoc potest videre, quis potest pati,
nisi impudicus et vorax et aleo?

That is directed at Caesar, who employs the man. The next lines give a picture of Mamurra at Verona:

> et ille nunc superbus et superfluens
> perambulabit omnium cubilia
> ut albulus columbus aut Adoneus?

Finally Pompey is linked with Caesar in a line that Rome never forgot:

> eone nomine urbis, o putissimi,
> socer generque, perdidistis omnia?

Catullus gave the epigram out at once, and as it reached Caesar very soon, perhaps a copy was sent to Mamurra or Caesar. Suetonius [29] tells what followed. Caesar knew Catullus well, was then the guest at his father's house—it was the last winter before Catullus' death. Caesar had stood much abuse without a whimper, but this pierced to the quick. He asked Catullus for a conference and a statement of the reasons for his attack, and Catullus explained. We are not told what the explanations were. We may suppose that he mentioned his aversion to Caesar's political course, but he probably also had something to say about Mamurra's behavior in Verona. Caesar accepted his explanation and asked for a reconciliation. I have ventured to use the word *asked*. Suetonius, accustomed to a century of Caesar-worship, put it differently, by saying that Caesar "forgave" him. When Caesar "forgave," the pardon was either well deserved or very essential to Caesar's policy. We happen to have in Cicero's correspondence a letter from Caesar explaining the advantages of forgiveness, and we need not go into raptures over his "generosity" on this or any other occasion. At this very time Caesar was, for political reasons, writing a great many "generous" letters (See Cic. *ad Quint. Frat.* 2, 13). Our only surprise is that after the reconciliation this epigram was not suppressed. Only a posthumous edition can account for its publication.

There is also an epigram against Caesar in a single couplet:

Whether or no I please you I hardly care,
Much less to know whether you are dark or fair.

It sounds very much as if this were Catullus' first answer to Caesar's request for a conference, but of course there is nothing in it to indicate a date. It is very unfortunate that another poem, also directed against Caesar (54), has suffered so badly at the hands of medieval scribes that the fragments left us contain little but misspelled names. Poems 114 and 115 are in my opinion directed not at the engineer Mamurra, but at the famous lieutenant general, Labienus, of whom we have frequent mention in

Caesar's commentaries. Labienus was from Picenum, which explains "Firmanus," and he too was enriched by Caesar for his services.

Enough has been said about the bitter epigrams of Catullus' last year. It is suspicious that they are so numerous that year. A plausible explanation might be that, young as he was, life had been too much for the poet and had embittered him. When, however, one reads such exuberant verses as the Septimius love-song, also written in this year, one may doubt the adequacy of that explanation. It seems equally possible that many similar epigrams had been made over the cups in verse-writing contests like the one at Calvus' house, and that an occasional clearing of the desk had consigned most of the early ones to the waste-basket, whereas those of the last year escaped destruction.

The Septimius song is also dated by a reference to Britain and to Syria. In 55 Caesar's expedition to Britain was common talk, and Crassus was fitting out an equally exciting expedition to the east, intending to conquer Persia and perhaps India. All the young men about town were getting letters of introduction to Caesar or Crassus for captaincies which promised to bring fame and fortune. Septimius like the rest has been hesitating between Syria and Britain. He visits his sweetheart Acme to bid

her farewell. Before the evening is far gone, however, he decides that love is enough. The poem,[30]
which Munro calls "the most charming picture in any
language of a light and happy love," is number 45,
and shall not be garbled by paraphrase.

It would be difficult to find a sharper contrast than
exists between this love song and the poet's last verses
(11) to Lesbia, written at about the same time. Only
the iambics to Caesar and Mamurra can match these
for agate hardness. Every effect is carefully studied,
even the use of the Sapphic meter which Catullus
had not employed since he used it seven years before
in translating Sappho to express his first love. I do
not think that his love had lasted these seven years.
There is no sure indication that any word had passed
between Clodia and Catullus after his departure to
Bithynia early in 57. The poems of love, the quarrels, reconciliations and final rejection all seem to
belong to the years 62-58. That the poet still loved
Lesbia in 57 is likely enough, but she had refused
him, and the scandals that came out in the prosecution of 56 he apparently accepted as true. The
eleventh poem, written in 55, seems to justify the
supposition that it was Clodia, deeply disgraced and
deserted by her friends, who sent a request for a
reconciliation through Furius. She had had time
enough to regret, and there was none of the old

Clodian pride left in her. But Catullus' love was
dead, crushed, as he answers, like a flower by the
plow share, and it was she who had crushed it.

> nec meum respectet, ut ante, amorem,
> qui illius culpa cecidit uelut prati
> ultimi flos, praetereunte postquam
>   tactus aratro est.

There is not one suggestion of pity. The long stately
approach to his theme through a conventional address—not to her, but to her messengers—leads the
reader unsuspecting straight under the cutting edge of
his piercing curse. We have mentioned the repetition from his first poem of the word *identidem* which
was just enough to remind her of *dulce ridentem*.
Such artistry is diabolic.[31]

To Cornificius, the unfortunate young poet who
later sacrificed his life for the cause of Brutus, Catullus sent a disconsolate plea for words of cheer (38),
and it may have been during Catullus' last illness,
since Cornificius was so young that an early dating
of the letter is out of the question.

> Male est, Cornifici, tuo Catullo,
> male est me hercule ei et laboriose,
> et magis magis in dies et horas.

He asks for a mere word of greeting:

> paulum quid libet adlocutionis,
> maestius lacrimis Simonideis.

This Cornificius, several years younger than Catullus, pursued a literary course not unlike that of Calvus though he attained to greater success in politics. Brief songs of his and a short epic of the type favored by the "new poets" were known later, and Cicero does deference to his prose style though it followed a trend opposed to his own. I have elsewhere suggested that there is good reason to believe him the subject of Vergil's elegy, the fifth eclogue,[32] written on the occasion of his untimely death in the civil war. His work is another instance of the widespread influence of Catullus and Calvus in Latin poetry.

Most of the occasional verses addressed to these friends were written in hendecasyllables. This meter was to the Latin ear not quite as clownish as Tennyson's parody would suggest:

Look, I come to the test, a tiny poem
All composed in a meter of Catullus,
All in quantity, careful of my motion,
Like the skater on ice that hardly bears him
Lest I fall unawares before the people
Waking laughter in indolent reviewers.

Yet their legitimate place among jaunty or trivial themes was assigned them by the triple trochees with which they tumbled off at the end. The meter precisely suits the deprecatory dedication of his first shy publication:

Cui dono lepidum novum libellum,

or the anecdote of his unsuccessful attempt to boast:

Varus me meus ad suos amores,

and the many invitations and missives of thanks. Because of its swiftness it did good service too in lampoons of the lighter, droller type, as in:

quare aut hendecasyllabos trecentos
expecta, aut mihi linteum remitte

and

Furi, villula vestra non ad Austri.

What must have surprised his readers was his amazing versatility in adapting this rhythm to any and every mood, compelling the reader to forget the conventional associations that usually clung to it. The explanation of this success does not lie on the surface. The patent sincerity of his emotions and the magic of his language would of course disclose his mood in any form, but the fact is that the meter itself assumes different tempos and rhythms to suit the spirit of each line. A close scrutiny will reveal a versatile adaptation of the variable first foot, a careful fitting of the central dactyl, and a variation of concordance between the quantitative rhythm and the word stress in the last three trochees. Whether or not this was conscious artifice matters but little; at any rate one cannot discover the rules of the game. Somehow Catullus has fitted this wayward meter to an unusually wide range of themes. In the pleading line:

> Vivamus, mea Lesbia, atque amemus,

an elision saves the complete coincidence of accent and ictus, as in the haunting:

> Orci, quae omnia bella devoratis,

and the inimitable:

> Nox est perpetua una dormienda.

The long word at this line-end, permitting the appreciation of the secondary accent, accounts in some measure for the lingering flow. What this means to the verse may be seen by contrasting the equally effective preceding line, with its sharp stroke:

> Nobis cum semel occidit brevis lux,

or the clash of the first line in the memorable couplet:

> aut quam sidera multa cum tacet nox
> furtivos hominum vident amores.

At times it is a sudden sense-pause that gives the required tone to the rhythm.

> Illuc-unde negant redire quemquam,

or it may be a recessive phrasing:

> paulum, quid libet, adlocutionis
> maestius lacrimis Simonideis.

However, such an analysis is as inadequate as it is impertinent. By suggesting it I have only wished to call attention to Catullus' disregard for the standard rules of his day which were very meticulous regarding the proprieties of forms and literary genres, and his ease in breaking through the restraints of a confining form that might otherwise have impeded his spirit.

The very first poem in the Catullian collection is a prefatory dedication of a small book of verses to the historian Cornelius Nepos, a fellow Veronese, written with his usual modesty. It raises the whole question of the editions of the poet's work. That dedication mentions a small roll, whereas a complete edition of Catullus would make three or four rolls. It must therefore refer to an early or partial edition. Its date cannot be ascertained, though the words *jam tum* would indicate that considerable time had passed since the poet began to write. This edition may have been issued in 57 before his journey, but more probably it was given out after his return. It

may well have contained the wedding songs and a
number of the minor poems. If issued in 57 it
would hardly have contained any reference to
Clodia; in 55 however a few of the Lesbia group
might possibly have been included since Clodia's
name was not mentioned. That the subject could still
bring torment to him even in his last year is patent
enough from the eleventh, and I find no proof in his
poems that his secret became general knowledge in
his lifetime, though various persons knew about it.

Some scholars find in fragment 14b a remnant of
a second dedication. This seems improbable for the
following reasons.[33] It has been noticed that poems
on similar themes are usually separated by a poem
on an alien theme: so 2-3 (separated by 2b), 5-7,
16-21 (nos. 18-20 are not the work of Catullus),
21-23, 24-26, 37-39, 41-43, 69-71, 70-72, 71-73,
107-109, and 77-78b. Now 14b seems to be a fragment of an *apologia* that corresponds to 16 in the
same manner. If 14b and 16 constitute such a pair
the former is of course not a dedication, and that
leaves the first poem as the only dedication we have.
The one roll given out under the auspices of Cornelius Nepos was, I think, all that Catullus personally issued, though of course many of his poems
circulated among his friends.

That Catullus did not issue the complete edition is
now rather generally accepted. We should not ex-

pect one so modest to include so many purely personal and occasional verses, nor so many mere fragments—for it is not likely that the sad fate of the
manuscript accounts for all the shattered ones. A
stronger proof is that the tirades against Caesar and
his friends appear despite his reconciliation with
Caesar. Finally the inclusion of a poem like 102 is
significant. In these lines he promises faithful con-
cealment of some secret. Since the poem itself has
no literary value its publication, which of course betrays the existence of the secret it would conceal,
must rest with some person who feels bound to publish every line he finds regardless of its content.[34]
The man, whoever he was, possessed neither taste nor
a sense of humor. Without any regard whatsoever
for chronology he generally classified the poems by
metrical groups, taking pains only to separate those
that were very much alike. This separation has
sometimes been attributed to Catullus, but if the
letter to Cornificius was written during his last illness its use as a wedge between 37 and 39 would
militate against such an assumption. Our conclusion then is that before his death Catullus had issued
only a small portion of his verse in a roll dedicated
to Nepos. What this contained we do not know.
All the poems were regrouped after his death, and
the dedication of the single roll was made to serve
as a preface to the several rolls.

V

EPIC ROMANCE

THE longest poem of Catullus, *The Marriage of Peleus and Thetis*, (64) is an epyllion, a miniature epic of 408 lines. It is the last product of his training in Alexandrian narrative undertaken at the suggestion of Hortensius and Manlius three or four years before. Yet it cannot well be called a narrative poem. It reminds one of a Pompeian palace-fresco with a mythological scene inside an elaborate landscape, or of a richly woven tapestry with additional designs embroidered over it. The framework is the happy wedding of Peleus and Thetis, while the central design, by way of contrast, is the desertion of Ariadne by Theseus. The outer frame consists chiefly of picture after picture. The central theme combines appeal to eye and ear, for at the very center the deserted Ariadne is described in an attitude of surprise and confusion, while about the figure runs an arabesque of narrative to explain it. In neither frame nor picture is any story completely told. Peleus sails to find the golden fleece. Out on the sea he beholds the nymph Thetis, and they fall

in love. The next scene is the wedding in the palace.
The next lines depict the tapestry on the wedding
couch with its representation of Ariadne, and the description requires more than half the poem. Then
back we are carried to the wedding scene, with the
guests bringing gifts, and the Fates singing the
prophecy of Thetis' promised child, Achilles.

The intricate interweaving of description and
narrative in the central portion makes an elaborate
and beautiful pattern. Ariadne on the shore gazing
in amazement at Theseus far off at sea is effectively
described. Then is narrated in rapid sentences what
precedes: why Theseus sailed to Crete, how she saw
him, loved him, helped him to safety out of the
labyrinth, and sailed away with him. Then we come
back again to Ariadne on the shore and her grief.
We hear her prayer and her curse upon Theseus.
Then follows the story of how her curse is heard by
Jove and of how Theseus comes to grief. A very
peculiar effect is secured at the end where Catullus
wanders off from his theme completely in subjective
comment: "Thus it was long ago when the gods
associated with men. Now the gods do not visit us
because of our sins." The list of those sins concludes
the poem and brings us down with a jolt to the days
of Caesar and Clodia.

So much for the artificial design of the epyllion

which is so foreign to Catullus' usual directness. The style also is wholly different from that of his short poems. The sentences are often long and they pry into the bypaths of suggestion by their loose clauses and parentheses. Elaborate similes, finished as independent miniatures, are worked into the setting by way of conscious ornament; far-sought words and epic compounds, rich in literary associations, abound. His diction, usually so lucid, becomes artificial and at times pretentious, though his ear for sound never deserts him. His usual style is purest Ionic; this is rococo.

The results are naturally of uneven merit, for the poet has here undertaken a work that calls for mastery in many directions wholly foreign to him. His descriptions, strange to say, are better than his psychology. The sea-nymphs rising out of the waves, the long corridors of the palace, the simile of the departing guests, the romantic procession of the gods coming with appropriate gifts—Peneus, for instance, carrying pines, root and all, to plant before the palace—the realistic etching of the spinning Fates, and above all the statuesque figure of Ariadne on the shore, these are all memorable pictures. Ariadne's lament and curse, however, do not carry conviction. She is too much a refurbished Medea. Had not Clodia taught him more of what a woman might say? Or was this written before he sent his farewell to her? Perhaps Clodia was merely capable of playing a tragedy queen. Again one might reasonably expect from Catullus the creation of a real love-scene, whether in the meeting of Ariadne and Theseus, or in that of Peleus and Thetis. But he left this task for Vergil to do. Perhaps his own experience in love had come so suddenly and completely that he was not yet aware that the conventional love-at-first-sight of Hellenistic poetry was inadequate. His marriage song and the Acme poem show clearly enough that Catullus possessed the sympathy of a creator who can penetrate beyond his own experience. However the text is broken at the crucial line and may do the poem some injustice. If with Vahlen we may restore line 16 to read *illa alia atque alia viderunt luce marinas* we shall at least have Thetis on the scene for a few days. The phrase *identidem te spectat* justifies the belief that Catullus would prefer to have it so. Nevertheless the poem falls short in that scene. In the minor details too Catullus is occasionally apt to follow a pretty convention rather than trust his own intelligence. One can only smile when Ariadne, rushing in sad dismay down as far as she can to the water's edge, remembers just then to lift her skirt so as not to splash it. That touch is surely straight from Callimachus.

The art of the poem is of course Hellenistic,[35] but to what extent Catullus used a particular model is still unknown.   One line is a paraphrase of a Greek fragment whose author is unidentified.   Catullus had translated the *Coma Berenices* of Callimachus for Hortensius, and the letter to Manlius as well as the sixty-seventh poem are at least shaped according to late Greek methods of work.   Those poems belong to the days of his apprenticeship in the new style. The papyri have recently given us considerable portions of Callimachus, however, and this epyllion of Catullus does not resemble Callimachus as we now know him.   It is more studiously intricate, it dwells more decoratively over description, and it is more interested in romance.   Perhaps if we possessed the work of the lost Hellenistic poets who succeeded Callimachus and Theocritus we should find a closer model for this work.   However, Catullus was himself as creative as any of the Alexandrians and a truer poet.   If we may suppose that he now felt that his apprenticeship was over so that he dared go his own way alone, we need not hesitate to attribute these last developments of the Hellenistic type to Catullus himself.

The question is somewhat complicated by the fact that the poem seems in style and method to fall apart into two sections.   These portions may have been

written at different times and under different influences. Munro,[36] whose feeling for style in Catullus and Lucretius was far more reliable than that of
most of our source hunters with all their parallel
passages of insignificant phrases, felt convinced that
the Ariadne episode was written after a reading of
Lucretius had left a definite impression upon the
poet. Since Catullus and Lucretius seem to have
died about the same time and the *De Rerum Natura*
was not published for some time after the author's
death Munro's hypothesis has met with disapproval.
But Rome was not large in those days, and it is not
impossible to suppose that Catullus had the pleasure
of reading a part of Lucretius' unpublished manuscript, especially since Memmius was the friend and
patron of both poets. The reminiscences in Catullus' poem that seem most convincing are all in the
first four books of the *De Rerum Natura*. Memmius, to whom the poem was dedicated—apparently
with Memmius' proconsulship in mind—may well
have been given a copy of the completed part to read
on that journey. It is significant that in Ariadne's
song, from line 132 to 248, that is, in 116 lines, there
is not a single instance of the spondaic ending, which
is the one most striking characteristic of neoteric
meter, whereas in the first 120 lines of the poem
there are eighteen instances of such lines. This fact

might justify a theory that Catullus may have
started a poem on Ariadne while reading a part of
Lucretius and while having at hand an Alexandrian
poem on Ariadne which did not use the spondaic
device; and that afterwards when he had studied
Alexandrian metrical devices further he used this
poem as an episode of a longer one on the marriage
of Peleus and Thetis.[37] This suggestion is of course
highly hypothetical and is not offered with a view to
asking for its immediate acceptance, but merely in
order to point out a difficulty and suggest that in
reading the poem it is well to keep the mind alert
for changes in mood and style. In any case the
hypothesis of a complete paraphrase or translation
from one Greek work is not likely, nor is it probable
that the whole poem was written at Rome after the
poet's final farewell to Clodia.

But to return to the question of stylistic genres
raised by this poem, the reader finds in Catullus'
complete change of method a phenomenon more
readily paralleled in Latin literature than in our
own. Greek and Roman teachers took propriety very
seriously in discussing style. We acknowledge in a
general way that the story of Tristram calls for a
diction and rhythm unsuited to a Spoon River
Anthology. The teacher of rhetoric at Rome strove
above all things to inculcate in his pupils a quick

feeling for the types that belonged to various themes. The political, the judicial, the encomiastic orations had their proper tone, and in passages of each there might be a place for simplicity and homeliness as well as a place for elaboration. It was a training which necessitated an intricate classification of types of literature and a correspondingly wide analysis of literary styles. And it was generally agreed by the time of Catullus which Greek authors best illustrated each type of literature. Naturally the teacher simplified his task by suggesting the study of typical models as examples. There was of course some danger that this use of models might lead to slavish imitation, but on the whole it was excellent discipline and the assumption was safe that while studying many types the pupil would find the one adapted to his temper and field of operation, and that if he had the divine flair he would soon break any shackles that the system might impose. The system did insist—and perhaps too frequently—that a well-trained writer should not be satisfied to be the slave of his own moods and that he could acquire the ability to employ a wide range of themes and adapt his pen to the appropriate theme, even if his chief work were later to lie within narrower limits. This is then a very old doctrine, though it now shows signs here and there of being on the point of re-invention.

In poetry the analysis had not progressed quite as far as in prose, for the reason that the Alexandrian age had been one chiefly of prose production. The epigram, as we noted above, had on the whole remembered its origin and had never gone far from its duty of subtle and restrained comment. It was Catullus who broke the rule and used it lyrically a few times, whereas Martial later sharpened it and applied a touch of aconite to the point. Lyrical poetry had suffered badly in the scholarly age of Alexandria, having—except for hymns to the gods —to take refuge in the gaudy clothes of the music hall. That type need not concern us. Catullus showed the true instinct when he went back to Sappho for his poem on Lesbia, but he lost his great discovery, apparently because he had in his youth grown so much more familiar with easier meters and found the Aeolian forms fettering his impatient utterance. The shorter poems that had been written in the literary world, Greek and Roman, during the century—the poems that Catullus read in the idle moments of his youth—were largely what we should call occasional verse. Modest in scope they eschewed comparison with the great lyric poetry of early Greece by avoiding especially Pindaric and Aeolian meters. Hendecasyllables seem to have been popular for drinking songs, poems of friendship and for slight anecdotes, the scazon was used for similar verse containing a sardonic flavor; for prettier themes the light and musical glyconics, for trifling verse on questionable themes the priapean gave the desired suggestion, and so on. Catullus, as he says to Manlius, had written such verse from boyhood, and since he did not then consider himself in any sense a lyric poet—it was apparently years before he thought his verse of abiding value—he wrote in the accustomed rhythms whenever the impulse came. Had he not considered it merely necessary utterance for his own sake, had he not recklessly or lazily continued to assume that he was the *pessimus poeta* that Clodia called him and that he called himself in writing to Cicero, he would not have thrown his most intense cry of pain into a measure that might to some readers suggest ribaldry nor written his most lyrical song of love in a rhythm associated with the mood of trifling.

It is not surprising that his friends, who must have felt the glow of his inspiration, urged him to attempt some more sustained work. To do that the standard approach was to write a brief epic on a Greek myth, one that had not been outworn, one also that would permit some "purple-patch" work

in description and in scenes of pathos, with if possible a pair of sentimental lovers coyly treated. The
best preparation for the task seemed to Hortensius
and Manlius to be by way of some translation—possibly of Callimachus. It was thus that Catullus suc-
cumbed to the urgent request to learn the poet's
art. The *Peleus and Thetis* was the final result;
we are glad to have it—but may well regret the offerings that were sacrified on the altar of a late ambition.

Catullus was not the first or only Roman to write
a versified romance, though his *Peleus and Thetis*
happens to be the best of the few that have survived.
Ennius had not written any, and since he exerted
a powerful influence in shaping the trend of Latin
literature, they were long disregarded at Rome. The
older and healthier poetry of Greece remained the
standard for many years. It was the migration of
young Romans to Greek and Asiatic schools during
the Sullan period that familiarized them with all the
forms that were popular in the Greek world. Among
the first poets of the new school, who are variously
called the *poetae novi*, the *neoteri*, or the *docti*, was
the strange literary vagabond, Valerius Cato, whom
we have already mentioned. He taught school for
a living (having been cheated, he says, out of a considerable property in the Sullan days), wrote verse

in the new style, and put out commentaries of difficult old authors with critical prefaces which later roused the ire of Horace. Catullus apparently was on intimate terms with him (see poem 56) though about fifteen years his junior. We cannot be sure that Valerius Cato wrote all his poetry in his youth. In fact it was only in his old age, ten or fifteen years after Catullus' death, that the young poets of that day made him fashionable by their vociferous devotion. Furius called him the siren who alone inspired and created poets, but Horace thought less well of him. His outstanding works were a "Dictynna," apparently an epyllion of the standard type, and a "Lydia," which may have contained the story of a personal love-affair. We are not told that he influenced Catullus, but in view of their intimacy it is probable.

Helvius Cinna, Catullus' companion to Bithynia and his comrade on the journey home, was certainly writing in this form earlier than Catullus, since the latter greets the publication of his "Zmyrna" in a famous epigram which speaks of the nine years of careful labor devoted to this one poem. The theme was the unhappy love of Zmyrna, which might provide psychologists with a counterpart to the term "Oedipus-complex." The poem was brief, but so full of far-fetched allusions that it soon earned the dubious honor of a commentary. It was such work that won the name of *docti* for the whole school. Cinna was certainly influential in shaping the literary ideals of the period, and Catullus greeted the poem with enthusiasm (in 95).

Calvus wrote the story of Io and Jupiter in the same manner, whether before or after Catullus cannot be discovered. Catullus refers (in 96) only to his friend's elegiac poem on Quintilia, his wife:

> Certe non tanto mors immatura dolori est
> Quintiliae, quantum gaudet amore tuo.

But we can hardly draw conclusions from silence for we should not know from Catullus that Calvus' songs, including a marriage song, were as popular as his own, nor, if the lone manuscript of Catullus had been lost, should we now be certain that Catullus himself was the author of an epyllion.

The other poems of this kind seem to have been written after Catullus' death. Caecilius of Comum had begun a "Cybele," as Catullus' greetings to him (35) give evidence, but we do not hear that it was completed. Cornificius, an intimate friend of Catullus, of whom we have spoken, composed a "Glaucus," but he seems to have been slightly younger than Catullus, and probably wrote his poem later than the *Peleus and Thetis*. Other poets who wrote in this manner during this period are mere names. Of Catullus' place in the list therefore we are somewhat uncertain. However, Vergil's dependence upon Catullus in his youthful epyllion, the *Ciris*, would seem to justify the belief that the *Peleus and Thetis* was later considered the standard model for miniature epics.

Catullus did not live to shape an original type out of this genre as he had out of the Alexandrian epigram. As we have said, he died at the age of thirty. There is nowhere a mention of his death except in the incorrect chronicle of St. Jerome. The latest datable event mentioned in his own works is Caesar's British expedition. Caesar landed in Britain on August 27 of 55 and remained there about four weeks. Catullus was certainly at Rome when he heard of it. Suetonius, as we have remarked, mentions Caesar's distress on reading the epigram on Mamurra and his successful effort at reconciliation. Caesar arrived in Cisalpine Gaul shortly after January 1, 54 (Caes. *Bellum Gall.* V, 1), and after holding his court sessions and making a detour into Illyricum returned to his wars in May (Cic. *ad Quintum Frat.* 2, 13). That spring, however, was long because it had an intercalary month of twenty-two days in February. It is to the period between January 1 and the middle of May, 54, that Suetonius' story refers. It is a curious coincidence that in the letter of Cicero just cited, in which he refers to Caesar's departure for the north, he uses a phrase which seems to be a reminiscence of Catullus: *oricula infuma molliorem*. This may mean that Catullus' book—apparently posthumous—appeared before May. We may, therefore, suppose that the death occurred quite early in the year. It was in February of this year that Cicero mentions to Quintus the posthumous work of Lucretius. Apparently only a few weeks separated the passing of Rome's two most original poets.

The vicissitudes of Catullus' volume were as strange as the poet's own adventures. *Pro captu lectoris habent sua fata libelli,* and Catullus' libellum provided none of the moral precepts, the standard meters, the rhetorical phrasing or the salacious stories that attracted medieval readers. Everywhere but in his native town of Verona he had been forgotten before the tenth century. There, however, the pugnacious bishop Rather, who made a point of increasing the store of pungent diction which so often brought him into trouble, found and used a copy which he mentions in the year 965 A.D. Then we hear no more of Catullus for over three centuries. About 1300 two Paduan scholars refer to him, having apparently found Rather's old copy that had been carried away from Verona. Then about 1314, Can Grande, the magnificent dictator of Verona, seems to have heard of the manuscript and had it brought home from its exile.[38] That at least seems to me the meaning of the three enigmatical couplets which Benvenuto, the friend of Can Grande, scribbled on the last page of the manuscript. During the next fifty years only Petrarch and a Veronese friend of his mention the manuscript, but Petrarch's references to it aroused some interest, and two copies of it were made before it was irretrievably lost. One, which seems to have been Petrarch's, found its way to Venice and came to light at Oxford some sixty years ago. The other was lost, but not until two new copies were made from which Renaissance scholars could transcribe copies of their own. On such a slender thread hung for centuries the fate of Catullus' precious volume.

VI

TRANSITION

CATULLUS and Lucretius died at the turning of Rome's long road. In the same year another person died who held in her hand more strands of fate than men then could know. It was Julia, daughter of Caesar, wife of Pompey, whose gentle presence alone, after the death of Crassus, had bound together in amity two powerful men who were too ambitious to share an empire. Very soon after Julia's death the rupture came which led to civil war and to the eventual victory and autocracy of Caesar. A century or so later—we do not know the exact date—the author of the essay *On the Sublime* raised the question of why Roman literature had then decayed. He pretends to think that wealth, leading to indolence and a taste for luxurious living, in some measure accounts for it, but he has another explanation also for which he seems afraid to assume personal responsibility and which he therefore puts into quotation marks as being offered to him by a philosopher.[1] It is this: "In these days we seem to be schooled from childhood in utter servility, swaddled, I might say,

115

from the tender infancy of our minds in servile ways and practices. We never drink from the fairest and most fertile source of literature, which is freedom, and therefore we come to show a genius for nothing but flattery."

That is not the whole explanation either, but it has substance enough to make it worth repeating. Caesar and Augustus were not men who actually suppressed freedom of speech. The traditions of liberty were very strong during the Roman republic and it took generations of the imperial régime before men actually felt any restraining hand. But for all that, the turn of political events did gradually and unobtrusively alter men's outlook, their interests, their occupations and their motives, until a change is noticeable that can legitimately be ascribed to the revolution. To be sure the golden age of poetry came in the days of Augustus and partly because of the encouragement of Augustus, but it is a debatable question whether the source of the inspiration would not have been clogged had Vergil and Horace been born twenty years later than they were. Both were old enough to know from experience the spirit of the republic, both owed their first impulses to the work of Catullus and Lucretius, and both were strong and creative enough to resist unwholesome enticements.

I wish in this chapter to sketch the story of the literary activity at Rome from the death of Catullus through the tense fifteen years of civil wars, when men were generally too distracted to think of the arts, to the time after Philippi when Horace began to write. Calvus survived Catullus some eight years. As in the case of Catullus, Memmius and Furius, Caesar made friendly overtures to him. The great general was so sensitive to literary expression that he estimated the effect of hostile pasquinades even more highly than the writers of them did. And he was an exceedingly attractive man when he desired to be. The campaign of epigrams therefore came to an end soon after Catullus' death. But a strange accident occurred, if accident it was, for some one close to Catullus published all the epigrams discoverable —even those that Caesar had humbled himself to suppress, and the volume distinctly involved Calvus as well. After the publication of the book the stigma on Caesar's name remained for all time. It is clear that no one in the court of Caesar could hazard to carry a copy of Catullus about without risk of offending. It became a polite duty, in the society of the court at least, to ignore and belittle Catullus, and it remained so even in the court of Caesar's heir, Augustus. Not that Catullus was not widely read, but his influence on the next generation was nevertheless somewhat curtailed. That itself was not a wholesome thing for literature. Calvus, the boon companion of Catullus, whose lampoons were in general circulation, suffered somewhat with him. While Caesar had made a peace which stopped future attacks, it is significant that though Calvus was considered one of the most important men of the Roman bar, he did not attain to any political office. On the other hand Calvus' prose style was very highly esteemed and his reputation as a stylist profited inadvertently very much from Caesar's ascendency. This question touches at several points the discussion of classical ideals which deeply concerned the poets of the early Augustan age and we must consider it briefly here.

The elaborate periodic prose of Cicero is of course one of the great artistic creations of past literature. It was accepted as the unquestioned model before Caesar came to power. It had grown up naturally with an aristocratic society. For centuries questions of state were debated in the governing senate, made up of the representatives of the aristocratic families who spent their lives in law making, administration and diplomacy. It was a body that demanded the constant exercise of accurate thought and deep learning, of well-based argument and a dignified presentation of grave proposals. The courts of Rome were the first training ground of these nobles, for up-starts found no place to plead where the life and liberty of Roman citizens were concerned. Here too the jury had long consisted wholly of senators, and even after several liberal reforms, of senators and knights, and accordingly speeches could not be slip-shod. The trials however were held in the open air of the forum and large crowds were constantly pres-ent to hear the speeches of prosecution and defence, thereby inviting the orator to a free display of emo-tional appeal. It is through such practices that the Latin language of oratory attained its gravity and dignity and, aided by an inflected linguistic structure that provided an abundance of resounding vowels and an accentual system based upon carefully measured quantity which invited prose rhythm, it attained to an unprecedented sonority. In the mouth of Cicero, whose sense of sound and rhythm was flawless, whose packed memory was ready with all stylistic resources, whose facile wit and immediate response to his audience enabled him to mold the language to any effect, this aristocratic prose became a consummate work of art.

But as we have already remarked, the fall of the senate forboded the doom of that orotund style. Caesar first insisted upon the keeping and the pub-lication of the senatorial minutes so that the people could learn day by day what the senators talked about. The persuasive periods were not copied down, only the gist of the speech, and it soon dawned upon the orators that if the populace read the minutes they would be judged outside by what they said and not by how they said it. Speeches became shorter and took on a more liberal tone in order to please the populace. Then Caesar began to disregard the senate and to carry legislative proposals directly to the people. After a few years a law was passed limiting the length of speeches at court trials so as to expedite the business of the tribunals. Finally the time came during the dictatorship of Caesar when speeches were but seldom called for: Caesar wrote out his bills in finished form, read them to the assembly for a yes and no vote without discussion. Thus the mighty organ of Ciceronian prose was silenced.

Rhetoric still continued to be studied during all this period because of the firm traditions established in the schools. But there were several young men like Calvus who scented the meaning of what was happening; and whether from a natural bent, from theoretical grounds, or in response to existing conditions, they practiced and advocated what was called the "plain style." Now the plain, matter-of-fact presentation had an honorable justification in old theories which we cannot review here. The schools of rhetoric conducted by Stoic teachers condemned extraneous adornment as false, and men like Brutus were to some extent influenced by the Stoic tradition. Epicurean teachers belittled rhetorical training as un-scientific and therefore favored a matter-of-fact de-livery. And the Peripatetic teachers deriving from and developing the critical dicta of Aristotle recog-nized the suitability of the plain as well as the elaborate style on occasion, accepting both on the principle of propriety. At Rome furthermore there had always been some powerful statesmen of the realistic type who were far more concerned with facts than with presentation, with deeds rather than words. Cato's response to the question of doctrine had been: "Get hold of the facts and the words will take care of themselves." Cicero took occasion to compare Calvus' "Atticism" with Cato's impatient bluntness, but perhaps only in order to suggest that Calvus was not so much of an innovator as men thought. There was after all a real difference. Cato's was a powerful mind using the natural re-sources of a biting wit, a penetrating logic, and a blunt and very efficient native Latin, while Calvus, according to Cicero, knew from theory all the arts of eloquence, studiously eschewed floridity and rhythmic architectonics, but studied the devices that made his simplicity effective with an art that always concealed his effort. That is, if we had his speeches we should probably find in them that amazing gift, so often revealed by Catullus' minor poems, of a seemingly artless and spontaneous flow of everyday words that produced an effect of utter limpidity and lucidity. The Mamurra epigram probably took as much nail-biting as any thirty lines of the epyllion, but in a cursory reading one is not aware of it. So it must have been with Calvus. Cicero who knew his art but never was quit fair to the Atticists says of Calvus that he filed the edge too thin; only the initiate could appreciate his art, the rabble missed it.

Cicero of course felt the trend of taste as quickly as any one and in his *De Oratore*, written two years after his return from exile, he takes occasion more than once to justify the claims of what he considers true eloquence. But he was not yet aware of the full danger ahead. In the year 50 B.C. when some very lively debating was in progress he was far from Rome as proconsul of Cilicia, and came back only to find that the civil war was on. For the next three years he was completely muzzled—in fact all decisions were then made by Caesar. When he began again to speak in the Forum in 46 he found a very great change. Great issues were never allowed to come up for discussion, the cases offered him were of trifling importance, and men were too busy to

listen to flowing speeches. Cicero became restless
and dissatisfied. He invited young men to study
under his tutelage, and he even wrote to Calvus
urging him to reform his style. He undertook to
write a history of Roman oratory, and dedicated it
to Brutus, who because of a natural inclination toward Stoic doctrine had in private conversation ob-
jected to Cicero's theories. The book was a defence
of Cicero's own views and a keen though generous
criticism of the younger group who had not heeded
him. It is here that Calvus is so delicately criticized,
perhaps with unusual consideration because of his
recent death. Brutus answered somewhat curtly
that his own point of view had not been represented
with entire correctness, and Cicero returned that same
year to the question in a more theoretical book called
the *Orator*. But his contest was in vain. Events
were fighting against him. He saw the futility of
further participation in public life and turned to
philosophy.

When Caesar was murdered, Cicero was again
called back to battle for the old constitution, and in
his fourteen Philippics he illustrated once more what
the old aristocratic style could accomplish. But again
the sword had the last word and Cicero fell. Then
there was silence in the Forum for years, but when
peace was restored and there was some room for the

orator at the tribunal and in the senate chamber, it was the style of Calvus and the Atticists that won attention, because of its modesty, directness and brevity. Asinius Pollio, who had grown up in his youth in the intimate circle of Catullus, Cinna, and Calvus, carried on the Atticistic tradition and was accounted the dominant critic of prose style, and the younger Messala, hardly less influential, followed the same course. One may safely venture to add that, apart from the exigencies of the times, Cicero's unpopularity in the Augustan circle, due to his last opposition to Octavian, had something to do with the ease with which the world temporarily forgot him.

In this brief sketch of a very important revolution, I have taken little account of the theories of the Greek teachers who were at the time advocating the merits of "Asianism" and "Atticism" against each other. The fact is that scholars have taken those theories more seriously than the practical Roman statesmen did. Dionysius, the Greek scholar, who knew the complete story of what had happened, states that Roman oratory was essentially a native creation, and that so far were the Romans from having borrowed their style from their Greek tutors, that they had on the contrary imposed their "Atticism" upon the Greeks. In his preface to his *Ancient Orators* written in the days of Horace he says:

"I believe that this great revolution (the return to a sounder tradition) was caused and originated by Rome, the mistress of the world, who compelled entire nations to look to her; Rome, I say, and her nobles, men of high character, excellent administrators, highly cultivated and of fine critical intelligence."

Now this shift of emphasis in oratorical prose between 60 and 40 B.C. has some bearing on Augustan verse and poetic criticism, though one must not press the comparison too far. It is incorrect to speak of "Atticism" in verse; but two patent facts need to be kept in mind. Firstly, literary criticism from the day of Aristotle to Horace had not specialized as much as now. Treatises on style or on a special character of style, as for instance on "Sublimity," or "Charm," drew examples with equal freedom from all fields of composition; lines from Homer, Sophocles and Sappho jostle sentences from Plato, Demosthenes and Xenophon. In Catullus' day, although men classified the literary genres with care, they ran their critical analyses in cross sections through all the genres, and it is therefore legitimate to assume that any theory of style adopted for prose might (though it need not) be applied to verse compositions. The second pertinent point is that Calvus' prose style, as analyzed by Cicero, proves in principle to be based largely upon the qualities which we find so neatly illustrated in Catullus' minor poems, but which are largely lacking in the embroidered-tapestry style of Catullus' Alexandrian work. We need not attribute this wholly to the effect of theory. As regards Calvus' prose, a conscious theory was in a measure operative, but we seem to be justified in attributing greater importance to the exigencies of public life and to Calvus' own temper than to theory. And it was not for nothing that Catullus and Calvus were so sympathetic and remained the closest of friends through all the strange vicissitudes of their brief years together. They were apparently of the same temperament. So we must say of Catullus' style in the minor poems, while there was a conscious theory to satisfy, partly exemplified by his Greek elder, Philodemus, the demands of his own nature were the dominant element. Theory alone is helpless in attempting to accomplish with simple means such amazing effects as *Miser Catulle* or *Quis hoc potest videre*.

However, what we wish to emphasize is that criticism could later shape a uniform theory of verse on a study of the combined products of the two men, the orations of Calvus and the minor verse of both Catullus and Calvus. And that is apparently what happened. When Varius later bids Vergil prune out a Greek conceit, and when Quintilius acts as Horace's

mentor, urging reserve, the use of the knife, the
wisdom of suppression—for nine years if need be—
when Vergil praises Pollio for his classic style in his
tragedy, when Horace criticizes the careless effusions
of Lucilius, devotes endless effort to filing his own
odes, and finally in his *Ars Poetica* emphasizes
above everything the need of restraint, clarity and
propriety, this means that the influence of Catullus
and Calvus continued to be a vital force in the
Augustan day. And even if Horace speaks slight-
ingly of the two men, that does not disprove the
point. Horace was somewhat too young to come
directly under the charm of these men, furthermore
their bitter attacks upon Caesar had somewhat destroyed their popularity, and finally Catullus and
Calvus had both made the mistake of breaking their
own tradition by attempting Alexandrian epyllia
which later fell out of favor and weakened their influence. But for all that, young men like Varus,
Pollio and Varius Rufus, who avoided the Alexandrian aberration and remained loyal to the earlier
style, carried the excellent traditions over into the
Augustan age. Although both Horace and Vergil
followed their own course with an independence
which precludes the idea of imitation, their debt to
Calvus and Catullus is unmistakable.

In verse writing, the production through the pe-

riod of the civil wars was not large. Whether
Calvus composed after Catullus' death we do not
know, but he must have had leisure during his en-
forced retirement. He died early in 46.[2] Cinna
and Cornificius lived on for a while, and Vergil was
influenced by both of them. Cinna may be the poet
who was slain by the mob at Caesar's funeral.
Plutarch says that he was mistaken for a praetor
who had been hostile to Caesar. This is possible,
though he might have fared as badly if recognized
as one of the group that had lampooned Caesar. His
epyllion was completed before 54, and we have no
sure evidence of later work. His propempticon to
Pollio belongs to 56, the year he was in Bithynia.
Vergil honors him in his ninth eclogue, probably
after his death, and Valgius Rufus praises him about
the same time. Cornificius lived twelve years after
Catullus' death, but was very busy in administrative
work. If Vergil's Daphnis (Eclogue V) refers to
him, however, there may have been time for some
literary work as well.

Furius Bibaculus wrote much—even an epyllion
on the theme of Memnon—and lived longest of the
group, for his two epigrams on Valerius Cato belong
to the critic's old age, about 40-35 B.C. A minor
scholiast considers him the subject of Horace's sixth
epode, which is a defense of Vergil. If this is cor-

rect he was a hostile critic of both Vergil and Horace. Furius, therefore, while carrying neoteric traditions into the Augustan age, must be viewed as one who did not influence the new generation except by opposition. Another neoteric poet of the transition is the author who wrote under the pseudonym of Ticidas. We have a pretty line of his from a wedding hymn in glyconics which betrays a Catullian rhythm. We have also an epigram of his in honor of Valerius Cato, the hierophant of the group in this later day. What Augustans thought of him we may gather from Messala's sharp sentence: "I do not concern myself with Furius, not even with Ticidas or the grammarian Cato." His mistress "Perilla" whom he later married was a Metella, possibly, says Münzer,[3] a daughter of Metellus and Clodia! Was she a *matre pulchra filia pulchrior*, and did she go the way of her mother, while Ticidas emulated Catullus in something besides verse rhythms? Ticidas, as I have suggested elsewhere, seems to be the son of the great tragedian Aesopus and the *filius Aesopi* whom Horace satirizes for his extravagance. He is indeed a connecting link between the two poets, but can have had only a negative influence upon the famous Augustans. Ovid, however, refers to him with some respect. Other poets like Varro of Atax and Anser are too shadowy to give us tangible clues to literary movements, and Cassius Parmensis, who wrote not only Lucilian satire but also epigrams and elegies, wrecked his career and influence by taking part in the Ides of March and Philippi. After twelve years of opposition to Octavian he was put to death by imperial orders and very soon forgotten.

That the influence of Catullus' later Alexandrian compositions was still potent in the forties is most apparent in the early efforts of Vergil. This young man, also from the Transpadane region, was a little over fifteen when the books of Lucretius and Catullus appeared, but he shows the deep impress of both almost throughout his life. The *Culex,* a very uninspired early effort, is cast in the form of an epyllion but because of its theme it gives little scope to the Catullian mood. The *Ciris,* written about 48-7 and not completed till about 42, is not only modeled on the epyllic form but has numerous verbal reminiscences of the *Peleus and Thetis*—and perhaps also of the *Dictynna* of Valerius Cato and the *Zmyrna* of Cinna. Reminiscences of those poets would be included if only as compliments to two authors still living. What is significant here is that, though Vergil also shows Catullian influence in his minor verse, the *Catalepton,* it is the romantic narrative form which invites him to serious poetry. This was well, for Vergil's was not a lyric temperament. It was in narrative verse that he felt most at home, a narrative form however that sought its effects not so much in a Homeric rapidity of plot as in episodes of deep pathos and in scenes of brooding beauty. It is not surprising then that when others were turning away from Catullus' less successful manner, Vergil, recognizing his own proclivities, used it as a model. Its meretricious artifice he had the taste to reject; what he could learn from it in deepening his feeling for human suffering, in enlarging his vocabulary of emotion and of color he knew how to take and use. That he felt some danger in following an episodic form is clear from the fact that he soon turned to the pastoral where he could indulge his mood with less harm, and then to the Georgics where his love for nature could be satisfied without the temptation to yield to extravagance. He abandoned the epyllion for the pastoral at about the time that Horace arrived from Philippi and began to write satires.

Another poet from the North, the Celt, Cornelius Gallus, succeeded in reviving Alexandrianism for a season. He began to write about ten years after Catullus' death, and, apparently inspired by Catullus' subjective elegies, studied Euphorion, secured the aid of Parthenius to gather for him romantic themes from Greek legends, and wrote four books of love-elegies in a new syncretic manner which Propertius, Tibullus and Ovid later followed. He very soon attracted the attention of Vergil, but failed to interest Horace. The object of his song was the actress Cytheris whom Cicero and Vergil both mention. This original poet might have done much for Roman poetry, but while in command of Egypt he disobeyed imperial orders, and falling into disgrace, committed suicide. His work suffered not a little in popularity because of this. The influence of the court even thus early is apparent in the disfavor which his poetry met at Rome.

In reviewing this list of poets we note that the civil confusion of the times militated against literary creation. The leaders of the neoteric group were dead and their influence partly weakened by their political apostasy; the members of this school who lived on for a while—Cinna, Furius, Cato, Cornificius and Cassius—were not men of great prestige, and most of them belonged to the political opposition; the younger men were experimenting, but were somewhat distracted by the cleavage they found in the neoteric compositions: the natural, plain, sincere style on the one hand, elaborate and ornate Alexandrianism on the other. It was Horace more than any one else who decided which of these two paths Roman literature should take.

VII

HORACE, THE REPUBLICAN

HORACE—Quintus Horatius Flaccus—was born nineteen years after Catullus, he was eleven when Catullus died and he began to write thirteen years thereafter.[1] But, as we have noticed, these years fell in a period of rapid changes which were bringing on a reaction against republican poetry. Our own literature can provide many similar instances of one generation revolting from the ideals of the one immediately preceding it.

Venusia, Horace's birthplace, is almost as far south of Rome as Verona is north; it was as much colored by the old Greek culture of Magna Graecia as Verona was by the barbarian customs on its borders. Horace's native language was Latin, for Venusia had been a Latin colony since about 291 B.C., but we are not sure of his parentage. He tells us repeatedly that his father was a freedman, which means that he had been a war-captive or a slave. Since Horace speaks of Apulians and Lucanians as being of kindred stock the presumption is that his father or one of his ancestors had been taken prisoner of war in the

Samnite or possibly in the Social War. In the latter, Venusia had made the mistake, though a Latin colony, of joining the Marsic rebellion against Rome. The city was accordingly stormed in 89 B.C. by Metellus, who took 3000 of its citizens captive. When the war finally ended in a compromise the Venusians were given citizenship with the Horatian *tribus*, and it is not an impossible suggestion that Horace derived his name from this ward.

Venusia was, like all Italian municipalities, a county as well as a city; it included a large rural district and the tone of the place was largely determined by the farming population, that is, by people who in this case were chiefly descendants of the early colonists. The language of the place, as in most colonial regions, was conservative, and the morals probably conformed to the language. The earlier literature of Rome would have an abiding place there as at the nearby colony of Beneventum, where Horace's teacher, Orbilius, had been brought up on the older writers. The farmers of the region likewise kept some of the ancient Roman spirit of independence. Venusia was one of the very few colonies that signed the Italian declaration of independence in the year 90. It may be in a vein of fun that Horace attributes his early caustic style to the manners of his home town, but his readers would

understand the allusion. And later when Horace
asserted his rights to an independent life, to
Maecenas as well as to Augustus, they might well
have remembered that the poet had been brought
up not in the courtly city which shaped children for
conventional grooves but in that colony of spirited
rebels. Maecenas in securing for him a farm in the
Sabine hills seems to have remembered the poet's
upbringing on the farm whence he had often roamed
away from his nurse to lose himself in the woods.
The forests of Lucretilis more than once reminded
him of the wooded slopes of Vultur, that out-burned
volcano that towers over the Venusian plain.

But Venusia was not only a country town. It was
an important trading post on the Appian Way that
ran from Capua to Brundisium, Italy's chief Adriatic
port. Caravans of traders, bound north and south,
were constantly passing through from Brundisium,
Beneventum and the Greek Tarentum. There was
enough Greek spoken in the city for children of his
day to acquire the language and some interest in the
manners of the Greeks. Perhaps it is due to early
associations in the trading-town that we find in all
of Horace's writings an un-Roman interest in mer-
chants and men of affairs. Many of his illustrations
of human behavior are derived from the behavior
of trading people, people of whom Catullus and

Lucretius are hardly aware. But Venusia left memories of other things as well. When victorious armies came back from the eastern provinces they marched through Venusia with their spoils. Proconsuls and envoys bound for Greece or Egypt or Asia spent the night there with their numerous retinues of young nobles. Horace may have paid little attention to Memmius, Catullus and Cinna, when they passed through, for they were a quiet company, but he could hardly have missed—though only eight years old— the noisy celebration which greeted Cicero on the return from his exile in 57. Such sights on the Appian Way must have drawn many of the Venusian lads Rome-wards.

Horace's father was not a rich man, but he was fairly well to do. He had a farm, but, not belonging to the small-town aristocracy, he did not have to limit himself to the modest returns of his land. He could engage in business as well. He set up a bank for the discounting of notes, a business in which there was naturally much profit in a town through which many traders passed. When his son outgrew the primary school at Venusia, the devoted father quit business, and took his son to Rome to further his education. It is an appealing picture we glimpse of the two cronies there.[2] Money for a pretentious establishment there was not. But the boy must have the best of teachers and clothes suited to his new associations. His schoolmates each had a slave attendant. Horace's father could not afford to provide one, but he himself took him the rounds from one teacher's house to the other, eager perhaps for the chance to sit through the lectures to keep abreast of his son's studies. Orbilius, his teacher of literature, was somewhat old-fashioned but distinguished enough to be the subject of one of Suetonius' biographies, of a marble portrait erected on the capitol of his native town, and of epigrams written by at least three poets of the time. He had come from Beneventum, was chosen perhaps because he might take an interest in a boy from that region. However, being a colonial he clung to the old classics—which Horace, therefore, came to know perhaps too well. One may judge from a lampoon of Furius Bibaculus,

Orbilius, ubinam est, litterarum oblivio?

that he gave short shrift to the popular poets of the day among whom Furius counted himself; and from Suetonius' sketch that he not only used the ferule on dull pupils, but that his tongue was very free when he interspersed his literary remarks with sarcastic flings at contemporary notables. If Horace's spirit of independence, his knowledge of old Rome and its

authors may in part be traced to these lectures, it is
also reasonable to suppose that his dislike of Furius,
Valerius Cato, and of Cato's favorite master,
Lucilius, and his critical attitude toward the neoteri,
then so popular, may be due in part to this courageous but caustic professor. And it is not surprising
that Horace proceeded from the lectures of Orbilius
to Athens to study literature and philosophy at the
fountain head. Orbilius was old-fashioned, but he
also protected his students from much that was short-
lived and trivial.

When Horace came to Rome and how long he remained there we are not told. Since he had been at
Athens for some time in the year 44, when he was
twenty-one years of age, we may assume that his
Roman studies had fallen between the years of
twelve and twenty. These were the critical years of
the great civil war during which Caesar subdued the
Roman world. The passing of great armies, the
comings and goings of the "deified dictator," the
magnificent triumphs, must have made a deep impression on the young poet as they did on Vergil.
But of all this there is no mention in his work.
Vergil, the Cisalpine, who had been thrilled by the
proconsul's deeds in Gaul, was devoted to his memory, but Horace remains silent. As Venusia had declared for independence in 90, and again in 43

favored the cause of liberty, the townsfolk could have had but little sympathy for the dictatorship, and Horace apparently shared the views of his own people.

At Athens again he leaned somewhat to old-fashioned ways, enrolling in the Academy at a time when Stoic and Epicurean masters were more popular. There he found Messala, the scion of one of Rome's oldest families, studying "Socratic lore" and he doubtless ran across the younger Bibulus and Cicero also, both sons of consuls. Messala became his friend for life; Bibulus he also mentions later with honor, but not the youthful Cicero, who spent his school days chiefly in jollity and living as he thought a consul's son should. The principal teacher of the Academy at the time was Theomnestus, a dialectitian who left no decisive mark on the thought of the day. Horace came out of his course of lectures a devotee of the Epicurean cult, converted doubtless by desultory reading outside of his course, though Plato always remained a favorite author. What was more important was his wide reading in the old literature of Greece and his experiments in composing Greek verse. It would seem to be at this time that he acquired his intimate knowledge of the best Greek poets, especially Pindar, Alcaeus, Sappho and Anacreon, not to mention the Hellenistic poets who were now popular at Rome. It proved an advantage that as a freedman's son he did not have to waste much time at declamation and rhetoric, for a political career would not have been open to him even if the republic had survived. His conscience was therefore free to follow the studies best suited to a literary career, and his poetry thereby escaped the verbosity that sometimes threatens even Vergil, and too often flattens the narratives of Ovid.

The news of Caesar's murder in the spring of 44 broke the calm of this student group, and Messala hurried home. Horace was less perturbed. To him it must have meant the removal of a dangerous autocrat, and the spirit of Athens did not condemn tyrannicides. In the autumn Marcus Brutus, the chief conspirator, came to Athens and joined the group, ostensibly as a student, but in reality to conceal more serious plans. Brutus and Cassius had been manoeuvred into futility by Mark Antony and had been forced to accept the petty office of grain brokers for the state, an office designed to remove them from the scene of action when Antony was ready to vault into Caesar's saddle. The two liberators had realized their failure and decided this time, if Antony should attempt a coup d'état, to save the republic if possible by a far more daring stroke. Cassius went to Syria where he was known to the armies and therefore had some hope of winning them to his cause. Brutus came to Athens, secretly planning to seize Macedonia, if the worst happened at home. That winter he assiduously attended the lectures of Theomnestus at the Academy and of Cratippus the Aristotelian, meanwhile making his secret arrangements with Hortensius who commanded the legions of Macedonia, and, contrary to his old habits of seclusion, inviting the friendship of the young Romans that he found in the lecture rooms. Bibulus and Cicero were republicans by inheritance, and Horace by the old traditions of his native city. When the news came that Antony had made his coup and had marched north to attack Decimus Brutus at Mutina, Marcus Brutus answered by taking over the Macedonian army in Greece. He engaged Horace and the other young men as officers to fill the places of Caesarians who refused to recognize his leadership. Horace became tribune, a position that would correspond to a colonelcy in our army, a very high position for one who apparently had had no military training. However, Brutus intended to raise and drill a large army in the East before striking, and Horace was certain of a strenuous year of training at once. The first months were spent in the cities of Boeotia, Thessaly and Macedonia, which he so frequently mentions in his verses.

This commission has been much discussed,[3] was even at that time, because there was a very strict custom that none but a knight could hold it, and an equally strict custom that a freedman's son could not be recognized as a knight. One of the serious objections to Caesar on the part of the aristocracy had been his disregard for such traditions, and it is not likely that Brutus, who was meticulous in upholding conservative practices, broke this tradition for his party. The plausible explanation is that Horace's father or grandfather had been a war-captive—perhaps one of the 3000 unfortunates whom Metellus took as prisoners at Venusia in 89. Romans were apt to make a social distinction between freedmen who derived from the misfortunes of war and those who had been born in bondage. And it is more than likely that Brutus found some such justification for his elevation of Horace to a high officer's commission.

Horace saw much service and not a little of the world during the next year. In the spring and early summer Brutus' army remained in Macedonia awaiting the outcome of affairs at Rome. When, however, Octavian deserted the Senate, demanded the consulship and made peace with Antony, Brutus knew that the war would be very serious and that he and Cassius must enlist all the forces of the east.

Cassius had now won over the twelve legions beyond the Aegean, but reenforcements especially in cavalry must be secured from the kings of Asia. Brutus accordingly marched through Thrace over the Hellespont and down through Asia, meeting Cassius at Smyrna in the winter. Shakespeare, using Plutarch's account, has made that meeting memorable. Horace later mentions only one incident of this long and wearisome march—a trial before Brutus' tribunal in Asia—but it is clear that he kept his eyes open and became familiar with many scenes that later flash across his memory. The picturesque snow-capped mountains of Thrace, the home of Orpheus and the frenzied Edones, of Dionysus and Lycurgus, are not mere literary reminiscences in his Odes. He had at least seen Lesbos, the abode of Alcaeus and Sappho, from the mainland, he knew the plains of Troy, the Bosporus and the Bithynian ships as intimately as Catullus; and the mere mention of Chios, Cos, Rhodes, Mitylene, Colophon, Sardis, Smyrna, and Maeonia brings to him precise and vivid recollections. To a later traveller he recalls these places as the scenes of his own strenuous campaign.

Quid tibi visa Chios, Bullati, notaque Lesbos,
Quid concinna Samos, quid Croesi regia Sardis;
Smyrna quid et Colophon, majora minorave fama?

And the lonely little town of Lebedus had struck him for some reason as a charming spot in which to live out his last days

The world forgetting, by the world forgot.

Our college students who have never even crossed the Atlantic find Horace's odes full of perplexing names. To him the names were not empty sounds. With rich literary associations they combined definite images of famous and picturesque places, and for many of his readers who took part in the task of ruling a far-flung empire these words were filled with content.

In the spring after the army was consolidated, the obstreperous Lycians and Rhodians reduced to submission and the cities of Asia compelled to "lend" vast sums which they never saw again, the army of seventeen legions, supported by Galatian, Cappadocian and Armenian contingents, marched back over the Hellespont and through Thrace—in no very hopeful mood. At Philippi in the autumn of 42 they met the trained legions of the triumvirs. Horace never mentions the first battle although his legion must have participated in the brilliant victory of Brutus and Messala, while Cassius was driven back and over-hastily took his own life. For several weeks the armies faced each other again. Then on

October 23 Brutus offered battle and was completely defeated. The battle ended in a general rout. In later years when it was all a faint memory and Horace had the good sense to include himself in an ancient joke, he refers to the day when he ran with the fleetest of them. Most of the survivors surrendered. There was nothing else to do unless one went to Sicily and joined Sextus Pompey who had taken to lawless brigandage. Messala and Bibulus gave up their swords to Antony and followed him to Egypt—for them a return to Rome to serve under Octavian in the presence of all their families was too much to endure. Horace, however, who was not a political figure, could more easily lose himself at Rome, and he accordingly returned.

The voyage back seems to have very nearly brought disaster. In one of his odes (III, 27, 18) he speaks feelingly of the storms of the Adriatic in November weather (pronus Orion)—this was the month the armies returned:

> Ego quid sit ater
> Hadriae novi sinus et quid albus
> Peccet Iapyx.

The 28th ode of the first book is a strange dramatic monologue of a man shipwrecked near the tomb of Archytas who, in expectation of death, begs a passing sailor for burial. The time of the scene is again

November (devexi Orionis). The suggestion was made long ago that the speaker in this ode is Horace himself. We may accept this interpretation without assuming that Horace had been so near death, for obviously he might for the sake of a theme intensify in fancy his personal experience. But it is nevertheless likely that Horace had had some good reason for thinking with a reminiscent shudder of the sea, and it is significant that he gives us none of the colorful seascapes that are found in Catullus.

If he returned by way of the Adriatic and stopped at his home in Venusia, it would not have been for long. Venusia had not been officiously deferential to the new masters at Rome and the whole territory of the city was expropriated by them to be given with the lands of some twenty other cities as bonuses to the victorious soldiers. Horace's father had apparently died; at least, a few years later the poet speaks of him as no longer living. The young man had lost his estate, which seems to have been nearly all he had. Some little money he apparently could scrape together, and with this he went to Rome to find some work that might give him spare moments for writing. Work, however, was difficult to find. Even secretarial work and tutoring were now generally done by clever slaves well trained for such tasks. Horace somehow obtained a clerkship in the state treasury.

By a strange custom, not observed in other offices of the civil service, the holder of such a clerkship had the right to sell his position if the candidate for the office was satisfactory to the department. Horace was able to pay the price for this post and to secure the proper recommendations for it.

Horace was now one of the thirty-six scribae quaestorii. Their duty it was to see that the books and records of the offices were properly kept by the slaves, to keep strict vigilance over the safety vaults that contained the moneys, the records and the laws relating to the finance department, to act as confidential secretaries at the meetings of the questors, and at times to accompany as secretaries the questors that were assigned to the financial administration in the provinces, the army or the fleet. The position involved some responsibility—indeed the scribes were required to take an oath that they would perform their duties with care and integrity—and it was not considered menial. To be sure, freedmen who wished to attain some recognition often bought such a position, but not a few knights who liked life at Rome, retired from business or from civil or military service abroad, to a position in the treasury. The office was often rewarded with a knight's rank and elevation to a tribuneship. For Horace it meant a possible livelihood and time in a garret during holidays and evenings in which to read and write.

VIII

THE SATIRIST

HORACE was now about twenty-four with an excellent liberal education, many bitter memories, few friends, and poverty. He had some little time for writing after much tiresome work. But we should hardly expect lyrics to come out of such experiences. The young poet naturally turned to satires and lampoons, following the example of Archilochus and Lucilius. It is not possible to be certain just which are the first productions among the epodes and sermones, but a few bear definite indications of date. The seventh satire is certainly early, a brief account of a humorous incident before the judgment seat of Brutus in Asia, the point of which is a rather flat pun. The lines are not sharp and the narrative is needlessly involved. The second satire is an exceedingly cynical comment upon the immoral life at Rome, especially upon the prevalence of adultery in high life. His sarcastic advocacy of courtesans as a cure for this evil can be matched in a number of present-day jokes, but most of the modern parallels display their cynicism in a more restrained vocabulary. I am not sure that Horace even pretends to be a reformer in this satire: he is disgusted with life and cares little what it all may come to.

The second epode reveals a mellower tone and a milder sarcasm on a pleasanter theme. It is a good-humored smile at idyllic pastoral poetry, and apparently at Vergil's.[4] A few years before, Vergil, when very young, had written a boyish epyllion called the *Culex*, which contained a charming if artificial shepherd's scene. Very little else had been published at Rome during the wars, and Horace apparently ran upon this while looking over the bookstalls. It somewhat amused him as rather unsophisticated. Horace knew the country, its peasants and shepherds. He had lost his own land, and he must have wondered what some city-bred soldier would do with the plot that had been his. The country looked very inviting, seen from the city, through the glimmer of pastoral verse—but, did this Vergil know what the actual facts were, or might not the urban reader take the poem too seriously? Horace writes his own version quite as glowingly as Vergil's —indeed with frequent reminiscences of Vergil's verse: the lazy carefree life with lowing herds, pruning hooks and wattled fold, the singing birds and babbling brooks, the fishing and hunting and milking

of the kine, and so on. And then comes his unexpected conclusion:

> Thus the banker thought to himself as he de-
> cided to draw in his loans and retire to the blessed
> life.—Next month he was back at his counter.

The satire is not bitter here; in fact the description
fairly runs away with the poet, and it was not meant
as a criticism of Vergil. It was rather a good-natured
suggestion that the banker Alfius—the ordinary city-
bred man—is quite unfit for the idyllic life that
Vergil had tried to make so inviting. It is not impossible that Horace sent his verses to Vergil with
an explanation of his own view of men like Alfius.
At any rate Vergil soon became his friend, and in his
Georgics a few years later and before the book of
Epodes had appeared, Vergil seems to take cogni-
zance of this epode of Horace.

In the year 40 there was a definite exchange of
amenities between the two men. It happened that
there was a bitter revolt in Italy against the confiscations being made by Octavian in the name of
the triumvirs. The disaffected elements secured
vague promises of aid from the consul, Antony's
brother, and took up arms. Since Antony did not
openly repudiate the movement, and since Octavian
set out to quell the rebellious troops at Perugia, it
seemed for the moment that a civil war might break

out between the triumvirs that would involve the whole world again. Horace in utter dismay at the pestilence of war upon war abandoned the satiric form and in the sixteenth epode issued a call to those who wished for peace to join him and migrate to the "happy isles of the west," leaving the wreckage of Rome to the blood-thirsty crew. There is no reason to suppose that Horace intended to have the proposal taken literally. The call was meant to suggest his deep despair and to shame the contestants into considering their duties as more important than their quarrels. Happily Antony hesitated till Octavian had captured Perugia, and then Asinius Pollio, who was Antony's representative in Italy, could begin with proposals of peace. Vergil was a friend of Pollio and may have known early of this turn of things. Having great faith in Octavian and in his diplomatic friend, he answered Horace in the famous "Messianic" eclogue.[5] To couch the answer in appropriate terms he adopts the imagery of Horace's call, which promised the joys of the "golden age" in some peaceful island. Vergil's promise is that under Pollio's consulship an era of peace will begin at Rome which will in time bring all the blessings of the Golden Age.

There can be little doubt that this public exchange of their views brought the two together if they were not already acquainted. To Horace the meeting was destined to bring a lasting friend and a new inspiration. Vergil was five years older, was now producing a series of pastoral poems which were attracting very much attention and were even being sung on the stage to large crowds by the Cytheris of Gallus. Vergil was a devoted follower of Octavian as he had been of Caesar, and was personally known to Octavian and Maecenas, who had saved his properties in the confiscations of Cremona. He also had a group of influential literary friends in Varius Rufus, Pollio, Quintilius Varus, and Cornelius Gallus. Before many months, Vergil with Varius took the young rebel to call on Maecenas, who if favorably impressed might in time become a patron and secure him leisure for his writing.

Literary patronage was far more of a necessity in the ancient world than in Johnson's day. Printing made it possible to control the sale of a first edition and thereby enabled publishers to pay something for manuscripts. At Rome every household that had any library at all also had skilled secretaries who could copy off manuscripts when copies were needed. There could in the circumstances be no protected publishing trade that could afford to pay royalties. Some men with literary interests like Cicero's friend, Atticus, kept skilled copyists at work, chiefly to supply to order copies of rare books, and such men would also manifold new rolls for the trade, but they could hardly afford to pay the author any reasonable amount since the very first copy sold might be duplicated next day by the purchaser as rapidly as the original publisher could do so. This is one reason why so much of Rome's early literature (aside from plays which were paid for by the state officials) was produced by authors of means who did not have to depend upon the returns of composition. Vergil —after his confiscated estate was returned to him— as well as Varius Rufus, Quintilius Varus, Catullus, Calvus, Pollio and Messala, were all men of some competence. Horace also had had independent means until the state deprived him of his property. He had now demonstrated that he was a poet of parts, and if given leisure from labors that left him tired out after the day's work he might well do credit to Rome. Since Maecenas had interfered and saved Vergil for literature might he not also interfere, as he doubtless could, in the case of Horace, at least to the extent of seeing that the state made some restitution to him? The result might be more difficult to attain since Horace had been a rebel and had not produced the fruits of repentance. But Vergil and Varius determined at least to try.

It is not easy to estimate the motives of Maecenas

in aiding young poets nor to state with certainty what was the full consequence of the influence which he exerted through patronage.   Maecenas was a rich Etruscan, very little older than Octavian, who had abetted and loyally supported the most daring plans of the lad after Caesar's death in 44.   For thirty-six years thereafter (till his death in 8 B.C.) he was Augustus' devoted companion and mentor, providing constructive ideas, advocating a firm but liberal monarchy, dissuading him from bloodshed, using every method to reconcile enemies to the new régime, and taking up any burden of administration without accepting office.   He was the ideal man as chairman of committees and especially of delicate diplomatic commissions.   It would be easy to conceive of his literary patronage as a device to win to the new régime the favor of skilful writers, a suggestion he might have drawn from the experience of Julius Caesar.   However the explanation of his generosity is not so simple.   Maecenas looked upon himself as a man of letters.   During his busy life he found time to write light verse in the Catullian manner, dialogues, a *Symposium* in which the speakers are Vergil, Horace, and Messala, a *Prometheus*, which seems to have been a discourse of an ethical turn, as well as other things.   He was a wide reader and showed a genuine love of literature.   It is not to be

forgotten that the literary men who were independent and did not need his material aid remained his
friends as much as those who received the gift of
leisure from him.   It is also a plausible hypothesis
that since he valued art very highly he wished to
encourage it because in his loyalty to Octavian he
believed that an artistic renaissance would in the end
redound as much to Octavian's glory as a successful
political régime.   Finally it must also be admitted to
his credit that he did not impose his own judgments
on the group.   Propertius, for instance, remained a
friend and recipient of favors despite his pacifism and
despite his stylistic divergence from the stronger
men of the group; furthermore Maecenas was himself an Epicurean while Horace leaned more and
more toward Stoicism, and while the patron wrote
verse in the Alexandrian manner, and in prose
adopted the extreme preciosity of the Asianists,
Horace preached classicism in and out of season and
Messala as vigorously advocated Atticism.   Every
opinion, every theme, every school found a hearty
welcome in that circle, so far as Maecenas was concerned.

It might possibly be considered significant that
Maecenas did not secure leisure for Horace until
(after some five years) Horace had ceased to rebel
and had accepted the new régime.   Maecenas was,

above all, loyal to Octavian and it is likely that active political opposition to Octavian cut him to the quick as nothing else did. But we need not suppose that he exerted pressure, or that such pressure would have succeeded in this instance. Horace proved time and again that he was very sensitive to the claims of independence. If one studies the era in all its political shifts, one realizes that Horace went through a period of conversion such as the most independent and outspoken of men—men like Messala for instance— were in all reason compelled to experience. The republic was dead; the only choice lay between Octavian and Antony, and every sane patriot at Rome soon made the choice of Octavian. Messala, though choosing Antony after Philippi, turned to Octavian even before Horace who now moved in the circle of Octavian's most devoted adherents.

The early meeting with Maecenas is briefly recorded by Horace (Sat. I, 6). Vergil and Varius introduced him. The young insurgent was of course somewhat flustered in the presence of the powerful minister and spoke none too fluently. He was invited to tell who he was and what he had done. The details were not impressive: his father a freedman of Venusia, his schooling, his participation in the rebellion, the confiscation of his farm, his humble clerkship, his verses. including his defiant call for a migration from Rome. Maecenas dismissed him graciously and apparently forgot him. But nine months thereafter he invited him into the intimate circle. The year after, when Maecenas with several important men from the department of state had to travel to Brundisium on a diplomatic mission to confer with Antony, he chose as his literary companions, Vergil, Varius, the venerable Apollodorus who had been Octavian's tutor, and our young clerk, Horace. One may imagine Horace in his dusty office enjoying in anticipation this month's vacation with the foremost political and literary men of the day. What conversations there would be over the cups, when the policies of an empire would be argued! It turned out otherwise. The great men were quite discreet; it might as well have been some fishing trip. In his diary of the journey (Sat. I, 5), Horace succeeds very well in conveying the impression of the conventional twaddle about wine, mosquitoes, rough roads, bad inns and a small-town boxing match. When he returned and all his friends gathered about him to hear the report of his marvellous vacation, he had very little to tell, and presently he jotted down his account of the succession of nothings as a joke on himself.

It was four years after this that Maecenas gave him the Sabine estate which enabled him to leave his clerkship and devote all his attention to writing. That farm in the hills twenty-eight miles from Rome was too far away to be of use to a man as busy as Maecenas, and the land was too poor to bring lucrative returns to an absent landlord. Possibly it had come to Maecenas as some other properties had come from confiscated lands that found no purchasers, or perhaps it was legally state property at the disposal of Octavian. That it had cost Maecenas any personal outlay we need not assume, and it is probable that he was gracious enough to have it deeded over to Horace as a fair restitution for the Venusian farm which the state had taken. The fact is that the triumvirs at that time still had the right to use state property as they saw fit and without accounting. Horace's letter of thanks (Sat. II, 6) was of course sent to the powerful man who had secured him the property, but that does not prove that it should not rather be thought of as a restitution or a pension granted him by the state.

But this is anticipating. We must still think of Horace as a clerk in the treasury, writing epodes and satires at spare moments and occasionally donning his best toga—a rather shabby one, Maecenas thought—to comply with the invitations of his patron. He was now sufficiently in the public eye to meet with critical scrutiny. He had "published" nothing, but his friends had copied and circulated some of the satires, Nos. 2, 3, 5 and 7, we may suppose, and doubtless more bitter ones which were later suppressed. His scorn for the Alexandrian style and his advocacy of a firmer, compacter, and more restrained manner of composition were apparently known from daily discussions, if not from some published satire which we no longer have. The surviving representatives of the Catullian tradition, men like Valerius Cato, Ticidas and Furius Bibaculus, were not seen in the gatherings of Maecenas, possibly for political reasons, possibly for social or personal reasons. Furius—if he actually was the critic who wrote under the name of "Bavius"—had placed himself outside of the pale; Ticidas—if he is to be identified with the prodigal son of Aesopus—was not the kind of man that would receive invitations at court, and Valerius Cato, the guiding spirit of these two, had made himself the champion of a lost cause. The Catullian school had sadly decayed to be represented by such writers as these.

But they nevertheless had sharp pens. Valerius Cato, once the doorkeeper of Rome's literary pantheon, was now engaged in his days of waning inspiration in writing a commentary on Lucilius. He undertook to attack Horace, the new satirist, as an imitator of Lucilius, suggesting that he lacked

Lucilius' personal charm and culture as well as his poetic grace and wit.[6] Horace answered with an exceedingly pointed and personal satire, the fourth, and again as the controversy continued, with the tenth. These are valuable documents in showing that Horace had from the beginning of his career thought out the essentials of those critical principles that he propounded in the literary epistles at the end of his life. In the fourth satire he says in brief: "Of course I did not originate satire; not even Lucilius did. The earliest Greek comedy satirized the crimes and foibles of men, and Lucilius harks back to them. I grant also the humor in Lucilius, but he wrote too much without an exacting conscience. He has not even style. As for my verses I never claimed they were poetry. They pretend to be mere talk in meter, as are those of Lucilius. To come to the next point, you say I write personal lampoons and have not the manners of that true Roman gentleman, Lucilius. But I have never criticized the blameless, nor have I written any of my satires for publication. Lastly I do not criticize for the pleasure of hurting. Your Roman gentleman, Lucilius, when invited to a banquet wrote a satire on his host and fellow guests— is that what you call gentle breeding? In a word my verse is quite harmless. I have simply adopted a pedagogical trick from my wise old father who taught me what to avoid and how to act by pointing out specific examples on the streets of Rome. I hope you'll concede me this right. If not, my friends will help me convert you to my point of view."

This answer is of course only half directed at his antagonist. It is as much meant for the public at large, or at least for the large circle of the older generation still devoted to Valerius Cato. I suspect that like the tenth satire it had some introductory lines addressed directly to Cato when it was first issued as a broad-sheet, but that these were omitted when the satire was adapted for publication. Apart from the general pronouncement, the pamphlet is interesting in several of its details. In the first place Horace seems still somewhat unaware of the literary history of the satiric form. He ignores Ennius and the late Greek "diatribe" and connects Lucilius with Greek comedy. Horace apparently knew more about early Greek literature at that time than he did about later Greek and Roman authors. This is an important point. Next, his frank criticism of Lucilius for his lack of meticulous revision reveals his own ideals of work, the insistence upon patient filing that has made so many lines of even his early compositions still quotable. Then Cato's suggestion that Horace is not, like Lucilius, a Roman gentleman, draws a rapid *tu quoque* in the word *Romane*

(l. 85), for in that word Cato himself is reminded of the fact that his own claims to citizenship had been questioned; and Horace adds for good measure that Lucilius despite his station revealed questionable manners in some of his scenes. In lines 65 ff. where Horace contrasts himself with actual prosecutors, I take it that Sulcius refers to Alfenus Varus (Varus = sulcus), the lawyer whom Catullus called Suffenus and whom Horace had called Vafer in the second Satire. In other words, Horace is referring Cato back to the really venomous lampooning and libelling indulged in by his own particular circle. The amusing ending, in which he explains his personal references by citing the methods of his father who taught by explicit examples, is of course pure whimsy. It gives him a chance to illustrate the method and thereby to satirize several other unpleasant folk: Albius, Baius, Scatonius and Trebonius. Horace is constantly offering some preposterous explanation of why he feels obliged to criticize. Later he claims that it is because satire is the only form of writing not already preëmpted by his friends, or because he is troubled with insomnia, or because he is descended from the pugnacious Apulians. He might as well have attributed it to the boredom caused by the treasury accounts which he so heartily despised.

Cato apparently did not accept the satire in good

part, despite its genial invitation at the end. He seems to have defended Lucilius with vigor and abused Horace roundly for his presumption in criticizing his betters. Horace answered this tirade with Satire I, 10, though he later removed the personal introduction and apparently rewrote the last lines to serve as a general epilogue to his first book. The main part of the satire probably belongs to about the year 37. He begins impatiently:

"That Lucilius is far from perfect is evident from the fact that Cato, most learned of all the aristocratic pedagogues, finds it necessary to issue a revised edition of him. [This is not only an unkind reference to Cato's own uncertain pedigree, but also an unfair play upon the double meaning of the word *emendare*.] Yes, I said Lucilius lacked finish, though I admitted his ability to raise a laugh, but that is not enough, for brevity is the soul of wit, as the Greek comedians prove. These authors, however, are never read by your imitators, who are constantly singing the praises of Catullus and Calvus. You say Lucilius has charm because he is full of Greek phrases. Would you accept that as a criterion for prose also? In my youth I wrote Greek verses but was well reminded not to carry owls to Athens. I write satires because it is the only field open to me. Furius is composing purple-patch epyllia,

Fundanius comedy, Pollio tragedy, Varius epics, and Vergil sweet pastorals. This is the only field not preëmpted by others. Is it so presumptuous in me to criticize Lucilius, when he made free to criticize Ennius and Accius? I gladly grant his wit, but I still maintain that if he were living to-day he would set a higher standard of finish. We can no longer permit slipshod writing at Rome."

Apart from specific answers to Cato's attack the emphasis is again upon finish, brevity, neatness and style, a style that the new generation must be trained to demand: Rome's literature has progressed beyond the crudities of its apprenticeship and is ready for a renaissance of classic taste. The true significance of these satires seems to me to be in the fact that our young poet, who has but recently joined the group that is destined to revolutionize literary taste, has already become the spokesman of the group. His program calls for pure diction, a fastidious taste, exactness, lightness and charm. He might have summed up his principles by referring to the ideals of the early Catullus, but that would have been misunderstood. He prefers to reject the work of Catullus completely.

From the same period of literary controversy— or perhaps earlier—comes a brief and very bitter epode (No. 6) which I surmise to be a defence of

Vergil against men like "Bavius" and "Maevius" who parodied Vergil's Eclogues and Georgics.

"Why do you snarl at innocent friends, you who run when a wolf is in sight? I am a friend of shepherd-folk, and I'll drive you back to the snows whence you came. You fill the woods with your barking, but when a bone is thrown your way you stop to pick it up." I should suggest the following reference as apposite. A scholiast [7] (who is not always correct) says on this passage that Furius Bibaculus is the "dog" in question. Furius came from the Transpadane region, and in Satire 10 is called "turgidus Alpinus" for his epic on Caesar (cf. Sat. II, 5, 41, and *Ars Poetica* 18). Horace here promises to drive him back to his home. Vergil would then be the "shepherd" to whose defence Horace comes. The bribe of a bone would refer to the fact that Furius, who had written invectives against Caesar in the Catullian day, later—for some material inducement—became friendly to Caesar and wrote the epic on the Gallic war. This interpretation would tend to identify Furius Bibaculus with the Vergilian "Bavius," a reasonable conclusion since the nickname Bavius means "barker." Since Horace disposes of "Maevius" in Epode 10, it is likely that 6 and 10 are companion pieces directed at Vergil's severest critics. If this conjecture is correct, it reveals

Horace as again a ready spokesman of the youthful group about Maecenas.

Horace, however, had to meet more than the literary criticism of Cato. He was frequently seen at Maecenas' home, where young men were known to congregate who had political ambitions. Maecenas' recommendations were influential with Octavian, whose approval was now quite necessary for any elective office. Men began to suggest that Horace who had held a tribuneship and now was accepted in Maecenas' circle would some day use his advantage and become a political figure. There could have been no great sin in this except that Octavian in order to appease the nobility had recently been careful to exclude freedmen's sons from the lists of approved candidates. Those who cared to criticize Horace for other reasons began to worry him with charges of entertaining ambitions which ancestral custom did not recognize. And the constant talk might also annoy Maecenas and Octavian, if it were generally said—whether true or not—that the government would pay with political office for literary compliance.

To meet this annoyance Horace wrote the sixth Satire, which must have been satisfactory to Maecenas, for such a frank statement, obviously involving both Maecenas and Octavian, could hardly have been published in permanent form without the approval of all concerned. The satire is so explicit that it must have quieted similar carping for all time. He explains that he has no desire for the worries of political office, and furthermore that he recognizes as entirely legitimate the Roman custom of employing in political office not only worthy men but men of families old enough to know and respect Rome's traditions. He discloses all that is necessary about himself and about his casual relations with Maecenas and, as is his custom, he takes the opportunity to deliver a few side thrusts at the petty foibles of others. Addressing Maecenas he says:

"Though a descendant of an ancient line you do not scorn the humble, nor do you grant favors to worthless nobles. You, wiser than the populace, know that men of unknown parentage have more than once served Rome with distinction. Yet the popular view in a measure agrees with censorial law and I should be the last to accept an office that is not mine. Why awaken useless comment as do Tillius and Novius? I, a freedman's son, was tribune, and am now your guest, and I am criticized for both. Whatever may be said of the first, the second criticism I resent. You are your own judge of your friends and I did not win your friendship by misrepresentation. When Vergil and Varius vouched

for me I told you frankly about myself. I am not
a criminal, thanks to my father of whom they talk:
it was he who brought me to Rome to the best
teachers, gave me all he could, his own constant care,
and his wise precepts, not once demanding that I
make a return to him by entering a career above his
own humble station. That father, so much talked
of, I prefer to all the noble praetors and consuls at
Rome."

The thrust at misplaced political ambitions in
Tillius and Novius, who wanted office despite the
censor's rule, Horace takes as a theme for his fourth
epode, as though to drive his point home. The
couplets are finished with extreme care and could
hardly escape being read and reread. No one had
used Latin with such biting edge since Catullus wrote
his lampoons on Caesar.

> Videsne Sacram metiente te viam
>   cum bis trium ulnarum toga
> ut ora vertat huc et huc euntium
>   liberrima indignatio?

Here was a fugitive slave, grown rich and powerful,
presuming to govern Roman citizens. After all,
Roman office should stand for something and Horace
did not hesitate to say so.

There is just one more comment on all this criticism, social as well as literary, and it occurs in the

ninth Satire. Horace had apparently had the best
of the argument and it was dying out, but a little
incident gave him the occasion for one more fling.
This time it was one of the neoteri, popularly called
the *docti* because of their obscure allusions, who dis-
played unexpected ambition and begged Horace to
further his interests with Maecenas. It was Horace's
turn to smile:

"I was strolling down the Sacred Way, mumbling
verses as usual when a stranger ran up and grasped
my hand.

X. 'How do you do, most sweet friend?'

H. 'Very sweetly at the moment, what can I do
for you?'

X. 'Make my acquaintance. I'm one of the
docti.'

H. 'The more valued for that.'"

Horace, taking fright, tries to escape. When the
leech hangs on, he remarks, "I'm going across the
Tiber, ever so far. I'm visiting a sick friend who
seems to have a contagious disease." The fellow
does not budge. Then comes the point:

"I'd like to meet Maecenas; I'm quite a social
figure, I sing the old-fashioned songs, and I compose verses with amazing speed. I'll help you push
your way up in court. I won't even mind bribing a
bit!" Every word is a betrayal of the temper Horace

most disliked.   Perhaps the scene is quite as imagi-
nary as when Ben Jonson uses it again, but in Horace
it sounds authentic.   It could not refer to Valerius
Cato or Furius, for these men knew better—nor to
Propertius, as has been surmised, for he was hardly
old enough.   It may have been Ticidas or some
youngster whose name has not survived.   It is one
of Horace's lightest satires despite its cruelty.   And
it seems to end for the time being the controversies
that met his early success.

All the while Horace was apparently performing his regular tasks as a scribe.   There is a reference in one of the odes to various dangers he had
passed through unscathed, and one of these incidents
is a shipwreck at Cape Palinurus.   I should surmise
that he had been sent as the questor's scribe with the
fleet which operated against Sextus Pompey in the
year 36, for the fleet was in that year overtaken by
a storm off Palinurus and a large part of it wrecked.[8]
We know of no other occasion that would fit the circumstances mentioned.

It was during the following year that Horace decided to publish a volume of his Satires.   Reserving
the Epodes for a separate volume he included the
satires we have mentioned and added a fairly dry,
sermonizing one on the theme of the discontent that
springs from a failure to set a worthwhile goal, as

his own father had (Sat. 1), and a bit of broad satire
on a popular gypsy, Canidia (8), on whom he also
wrote a coarse epode in the Archilochian style. Then,
since it was his first publication, he secured permis-
sion to mention the names of several men of note
who could vouch, as it were, for his deserts, and this
list he fitted to the last satire, No. 10, with a neat
joining. The device reminds one of the "foreword"
that distinguished authors now sometimes write to
help launch incipient talent.

Horace's list of notables is interesting from several
points of view. It begins with his immediate circle
—now forming itself into the new classical school—
and its supporters (Sat. I, 10, 81 ff.): Plotius, Varius,
Maecenas, Vergil, Valgius (writing elegies), Octa-
vius (probably the historian), Fuscus (he of the
pharetra) and the brothers Visci (two knights interested in literature). Then comes a new group, curiously introduced thus:

> Ambitione relegata, te dicere possum
> Pollio, te, Messala, tuo cum fratre, simulque
> vos Bibule et Servi, simul his te, candide Furni.

The striking fact is that all of these men had been
associated, for some time at least, with Brutus or
Antony. Pollio had been Antony's representative
during the Perusine war and, though now living at
Rome, was not of the court party. Messala had been

the cavalry officer of Cassius at Philippi and had
later chosen to go with Antony, and though he had
had to abandon Antony's party and accept Octavian's
régime, he preserved as far as possible a dignified independence. Bibulus was Brutus' stepson, now serving with Antony and coming to Rome only on diplomatic missions. Servius seems to be the son of the
republican jurist Sulpicius, while Furnius, also a
friend of Brutus, was now serving under Antony in
Asia. In other words, most of these men were old
friends of Horace in the days of his rebellion. He
has not forgotten them and he wants them included
among his vouchers. If this be the spirit of his
grouping we must interpret "ambitione relegata" accordingly. The thought that lies behind this phrase
is something like this: "You have gossiped about
my political ambitions. My mention of Maecenas
and the rest you will again use as proof that I am
canvassing for office. The following names I may
mention without incurring that charge." The whole
passage is exceedingly frank, but satire was supposed
to be that, and the inclusion of these names does
credit to the poet and even more to the broad political
generosity of Maecenas to whom the book is dedicated.

That first book of Horace's added something to
the connotation of the word *satura*, partly because

of his conception of the word, but more because his own temperament and the occasions that called for expression shaped his material beyond the scope of his own definition. In fact the definition of the word kept changing year by year with his own change of interest. The word *satura* itself does not occur in Horace till a few years later—when it is used twice in the second book, almost interchangeably with *sermo*, i.e. talk. The word *satura* had a peculiar history.[9] We need pay no attention to Livy's curious account of a putative early "dramatic satura" at Rome. Professor Hendrickson has shown the source of that aberration; and any scholar who will take the time to acquaint himself with the historical sources of the fourth century B.C. will quickly see the impossibility of any accurate survival of literary history from that time.

The word actually begins with Ennius who not only wrote annals, tragedies and comedies but a large number of minor compositions in prose and verse. The latter he gathered from time to time and published in rolls which he called miscellanies. His precise title was *satura*, a word borrowed from the kitchen. It was in fact a "dressing," or what used to be called *farce* or *force-meat* in English, not unlike the mixture used as a filling for roast fowl. The recipe we happen to have: coarse meal or bread crumbs, nuts (preferably pine-nuts, the *pinelli* so popular still in Italy), raisins, and as seasoning a dash of sweet wine. Ennius seems to have had in mind the necessity of using a word which would suggest a variety of palatable ingredients. There is in Ennius' *satura* no trace of invective, so far as we can now judge from the few fragments left.

Lucilius half a century later began to issue books of miscellaneous content, which, adopting Ennius' suggestion, he also called *satura*. The separate compositions, usually several in each book, contained table talk, travel sketches, anecdotes, literary, political, grammatical and moral comment, etc. In fact each volume was an annual magazine, as it were, written by the editor. From the very first, however, Lucilius' bellicose temperament revealed itself, and as time went on, the critical tone, often used with a corrective purpose, became predominant. Lucilius ranged from diatribe to sympathetic jest, from moral discourse to salacious anecdote, but generally with a free use of sarcasm, irony and invective. He was very fond of a laugh but it was not too often the hearty, jovial laugh that he aroused. Horace's explanation of this style by referring to Aristophanes and the old comedy need not be taken too seriously. Horace probably knew that the word had been used by Ennius, and that Lucilius had given a new stamp to the title by following his own mood. And it is quite possible that Lucilius had himself excused his custom of lampooning individuals by referring to the example of Aristophanes. But what concerned Horace most when charged with aping Lucilius was to find a *tu quoque*, and so he blurted out peevishly: even your Lucilius had his models which he misused. By the time Horace wrote his epistles, if not before, he knew Bion the Borysthenite as a typical writer of satiric discourse and possibly also Cercidas. Bion, a bitter and independent critic, a man who had, like Horace, met many misfortunes, had written numerous pungent essays in prose. Possibly Lucilius, who was very well read, had known him also. One may perhaps conclude from this late reference that Horace had just learned to know his work, and was offering a correction of his previous conjecture—or was he again suggesting that Lucilius was being too highly honored as an innovator? It was an age when reference to Greek models did little harm and proved commendable scholarship. We do not progress very far by following such leads. Lucilius at any rate had made a strong impression. Several men wrote commentaries to explain his personal references and allusions, and others, whose works are now lost, published occasional essays in the Lucilian style.

In a mild sort of way Horace was certainly an imitator in his first book. That he had in mind a continuation of the Lucilian miscellany, with a critical purpose and "satirical" methods, there can be no doubt. He freely admits it, and his experiences had been bitter enough to tempt him into cynical comment. It is likely that he gave vent to his mood at first in Archilochian iambics and that, finding this form too narrow in its associations, he turned to Lucilius. Horace believed thoroughly in orderly procedure in literature and in using a recognized genre which would give the proper clue to one's purpose. To be sure he soon found himself involved in controversies which did not lend themselves to the more usual style of narrative satire. In 4, 6, and 10 he is slightly off the beaten track, but he sticks to the genre even here by the use of occasional side thrusts and uncomplimentary personal allusions. When he comes to his second book of satires, however, his controversies are about over, and pleasant experiences have mellowed his mood. The caustic thrusts at individuals become infrequent, the satire broadens out over a generalized stage of imagined or mythical culprits, and the amiable smile is seldom far away.

For this change, as for the original impulse, we need look no further than to Horace's own experiences and his urge toward appropriate self-expression. I do not mean to say that Horace would seriously object to a statement that he borrowed suggestions freely from his predecessors. The views of the Greeks and Romans, as of the Italian, French and English writers of the Renaissance and of the eighteenth century regarding what constituted legitimate and illegitimate imitation were very different from the opinions of the present day. The scholastic insistence upon "original work" has so invaded the field of art that the artist is often prevented from adequate expression by the demand for novelty, and art is too frequently driven to spareness or grotesqueness thereby. One wonders what Shakespeare, Molière or Raphael would have done if compelled to submit to the demands of modern pedantry, always on the hunt for parallels, sources and models. As the *Ars Poetica* shows, Horace believed in well-established and proved standards and forms. They had been tried and presumably had not been found wanting. They provided discipline and prevented waste of time in non-essentials. After all, the greatest poets have found even the sonnet pliable enough for the deepest utterance. And what was true of form was also true of ideas and fancies. Horace would not think of avoiding the theme of a travel sketch because Lucilius had written one, and if in that sketch Lucilius described a storm, or an evening's entertainment or a brawl, that did not constitute a reason, as it might to-day, for avoiding the description of a similar experience if it had come his way. And to go a step farther, if in such a scene Lucilius had happened upon a graceful or imaginative turn of thought which put the matter at its best, Horace would see no more reason for choosing a less adequate turn simply because the best had already been used than a painter would for employing the wrong color because the right one had already been employed by some one else. The only demand is that his experience, his idea, his conviction, be thoroughly his at the time; that it permeate him and have full meaning for him. And if it does that, then parallelisms of form or phrase are of no importance.

This question of Horace and his "models" has been needlessly discussed.[10] We have on the one hand the claim of slavish dependence, on the other of complete originality. Neither will stand the test of investigation. The source hunters point to similarities of theme. Naturally within a chosen genre themes and form would be similar: that was what constituted a genre. Critics point out that in the diary of his journey there were muddy roads and a boat trip in Horace as in Lucilius—as though

Horace ought to have trudged the wagon route and left the barge for originality's sake, or sent a commission to pave the road so as to avoid Lucilian mud. At times Horace is so free in his references to Lucilius that he employs a type-name taken from his predecessor, as we refer to Hamlet or the Ancient Mariner as recognizable types. These are instances of the employment of literary reminiscence for the sake of clarity and compactness rather than examples of plagiarism. Critics also point to a list of words found only in Lucilius before Horace which fit well into parallel columns. However, since ninety-five percent of the literature of the republican period has been lost to us it is hazardous to say where Horace got these words—if indeed the matter is of any importance. Horace himself would hardly have comprehended all the pother over this whole question. He had written what he had to say, whether the first fructifying hint came to him from observation, or experience, or from pondering over a phrase of Lucilius or perhaps over a Greek diatribe; his work represented him in his own setting; he wrote in pithy, pointed, tersely finished lines, composed in a personal, Horatian style that no one could mistake for anything but his own. To him that was enough.

After the issue of the first book, he continued to write an epode now and then though he seldom had occasion to excite his bile to the seething point, now that life had become pleasanter to him. The satires of the second book revolve about more general themes and reveal a deeper concern for social and ethical problems. The second satire purports to contain the wise remarks of an old farmer on the advantages of plain living. The third, written after Horace had received his Sabine farm, pretends to give, with not a little skeptical raillery, the sermon of a Stoic on the theme that all but the Stoic philosophers are at least a trifle insane. The fourth is a burlesque of the epicure's pedantry over toothsome dishes. The fifth, also written after he had moved to his farm, derides the practice of seeking legacies. In form it is a burlesque on the scene in the Odyssey where Ulysses asks advice from the seer Tiresias. The sixth was probably meant as a letter of thanks for his estate, which was given him in 33, and contrasts city and country life. In the seventh, his own slave, taking advantage of the Saturnalia, undertakes to prove to him the Stoic maxim that all men—including Horace—are in some respect slaves unless set free by philosophy. It is in this satire that we learn that Horace is a knight and wears the ring of that order. The eighth is an orthodox satire on a parvenu's dinner party, reported by one of the guests. The first, an epilogue placed in the position of a prologue, is a playful defense of his persistence in writing satire against the advice of his shrewd legal friend Trebatius. He would write an epic on Caesar, he says, if he were capable, but he is not. And write he must. It is in him and must out. "The dog bites, the bull gores, Scaeva murders, Milionius gets drunk, all because they are born to that; I'm of Apulian stock and must fight." In point of fact there is very little of the pugilist left in him, and the prologue—hinting at a bygone controversy—merely brings out the general mellowness of the seven compositions that follow.

Most of these pieces were written after Horace had left the city to live with his books and meditations on the farm which had been given to him two years before the battle of Actium. The new home, which brought back memories of his peaceful boyhood life near the gaunt Mt. Voltur and of his sage father, had already begun to soften his temper. A trend, not wholly to be expected in Horace, now begins to make itself felt, his deep interest in social and moral questions. This was an interest that had probably not been encouraged by Maecenas, who was an epicure as he was an Epicurean, somewhat of a dandy, devoted to good food and to a very free pagan program of life. Association with Maecenas had not deeply influenced Horace, though the epodes addressed to him are not pitched in the highest moral key. Even in those years at Rome, however, even in the cynical second satire, Horace reveals a very real concern for Rome's morals. In this respect he is much more of the old-breed Roman than Maecenas. After his return to the Sabine hills it is the boyhood teaching of his simple and old-fashioned country home and the plain precepts of his father that begin to tell.

When one meets Stoic commonplaces in the odes, phrased to be sure with infinite neatness, the first impulse is to reject them as out of place in lyrics. The result is usually an impatience which does scant justice to their worth. They seem more in place in pedestrian *sermones* written out on the Sabine hills. In that setting one may see their meaning. To Horace's Roman readers they were not simply platitudes; to many indeed they must have seemed more or less insane. Five hundred years of expansion had brought immense fortunes to Rome and sophistication was breaking down the old rules of conduct. Life was joyous and there were few moral saws that needed to be respected. Rome was living riotously without fear of consequences. When Horace's father in the prime of life closed his bank and invested what seemed a meager fortune in order to live on the returns so as to devote the rest of his days to the education of his one boy, he had done a very uncommon thing. He was not an ordinary man. That Horace never forgot. To him it was not trite to say that wealth is dangerous, that it is well to limit one's getting, that there are spiritual values worth more, that natural desires may as well be curbed. When Horace speaks in this fashion and laughs at Rome's behavior he is remembering his father who dared to go his own heterodox way, and he is also parting company with the practical creed of Maecenas and most of the powerful men of Rome. From his own creed he never diverges—reiterating it all the more the less it is heeded. To one who knows Horace in his setting it seems a strange paradox that the authorities of the Middle Ages indexed him as immoral.

IX

LIFE IN THE SABINE HILLS

HORACE's villa as rebuilt and enlarged a hundred years later has now been discovered near Licenza on a knoll to the left of the road that leads up from Mandela. The remains have just been described in an excellent publication of the Italian Royal Academy by the distinguished archaeologist Professor Lugli,[11] who has also promised to publish an English version of the report. The poet's villa probably did not contain the elaborate annexes to be seen to-day, for they reveal workmanship of Vespasian's time. But the site gives us some indication of Horace's surroundings. The hills rise so rapidly on both sides of the stream that we are somewhat surprised at Horace's own account of the estate which mentions five renters of individual plots on it besides a staff of some eight slaves to cultivate the portion which Horace kept under his own control. The renters, if they were working peasants, would probably not care for more than fifteen acres each, and the working slaves would not take charge of more, but even so we should have to account for about a hundred and fifty acres of arable land, whereas the valley itself does not provide more than about twenty in this neighborhood. Presumably we must take into account the plots of land on the upper plateau, which have to be reached by going up the mule-path toward Monte Gennaro. It is almost a two-hour walk up an ascent of some 1500 feet to reach these small tracts, but that is accomplished every day during spring and summer by the peasants who farm those gardens now, and the Roman peasant was quite as vigorous.

In the center of this upland tract there is a splendid spring called the Fonte di Campitelli which gushes out of the Jurassic limestone ledge several feet above the path, or rather I should say it did so until a few years ago when the proprietor—whose name deserves oblivion—drove an iron water-pipe into the ledge and led the water down a hundred yards to a cement trough for the convenience of his lazy goats. Now this to me is the Fons Bandusia— at least it was before its desecration. I cannot prove it, but that cannot be helped. Any one who walks over Monte Gennaro knows that that is Horace's Lucretilis, and any one who sees the Fonte di Campitelli, and doubts that this is the Fons Bandusia is welcome to his doubts. Scholarly quotations of proof, syllogisms and enthymemes have of course no place on a page that treats of a poet's fountain. Bandusia

becomes a matter of religious faith to every devotee
of Horace. Others may have their own favorites,
the one at Venusia, which the poet never visited
again, or the prosaic one above his house that filled
his bath for him, or the plebeian one above Rocca
Giovane which has no better taste than to run down
along a mule-path. There is still time for such to
repent. I offer the following arguments for my
Bandusia not because they would convince me but
because proofs are expected. Springs are numerous
in the Sabine hills but they are generally nameless,
they are just *il fonte*. The one I refer to is the only
distinctive landmark for several miles in a lonely
district. It would have had a name as it does to-day.
Ask any man at Licenza or Rocca Giovane the way
to Gennaro and he will give you directions to the
Fonte di Campitelli and then on to Gennaro. It
must have had a name. Moreover this is the only
spring I know of that has the picturesque situation
and the generous rush of water that would merit
comparison with Castalia and Hippocrene. The
spring bursts forth from the center of a sheer wall
of limestone over which is a narrow ledge on which
grow gorse and a few trees. Thirdly, as I have said,
Horace's estate must have included these upland
tracts and therefore this spring was probably on his
estate. Fourthly, I believe Horace had a shelter on

the knoll on the side of Monte Marcone within a hundred yards of the spring. Numerous sherds of Roman roof-tile are still to be seen there. That was not the place for a dwelling; the peasants do not live there; it is too cold through six months of the year. They come up daily from the valley during the brief summer season to cultivate the soil. They might have had thatched shelters for an occasional night's stay, but such shelters would not be tiled. Besides the place is an outlook point on the coolest exposure. I am persuaded that the poet had a modest retreat built there for quiet composition and that his "bob-tailed mule" carried him there with his tablets when he wanted to get away from his grumbling overseer and be alone with the sprite who inhabited the spring in the days when there were no iron pipes. Here then are four plausible arguments which will convince no one. Tramp to the Villa di Orazio by way of Monte Gennaro and the Fonte di Campitelli, however, and then no arguments will be needed.

But to come back to earth, and the valley, Horace of course did not live at his villa continuously. He probably spent his winters in Rome and visited Maecenas frequently; but after he acquired his Sabine farm it seems to have been his regular summer home. It is there that he did much of his writ-

ing, enjoying a certain amount of exercise by taking
a share in the work of the garden.   Then came the
civil war between Antony and Octavian.   It is not
impossible that the 14th ode of the first book is
Horace's first expression of dismay at the rumors
that preceded this war in 32.   It would be hazardous to place any ode earlier than 32 B.C., whereas the
sentiment of the last stanza, in which he still refers
to the rebellious proposal of the 16th Epode, ought
to warn us not to place it later.

> O navis referent in mare te novi
> Fluctus.   O quid agis?   Fortiter occupa
> Portum. . . .
>
> Nuper sollicitum quae mihi taedium,
> Nunc desiderium, curaque non levis,
>   Interfusa nitentes
>   Vites aequora Cycladas.

Quintilian uses this poem as an illustration of
allegory, and assures us that it was the "ship of
state" that was thus addressed.   This then is our
first indication that Horace is thoroughly reconciled
with Octavian's régime.   The behavior of Antony
made him, together with so many others, a partizan
of Octavian.   Campbell [12] has a reasonable suggestion that Epode 7:

> Quo quo scelesti ruitis? aut cur dexteris
>   Aptantur enses conditi?

may also belong to this period, when three hundred senators who were partizans of Antony hastened from Rome to join in the attack. The old view that this epode belongs to the Perusine crisis seems to receive some support from the mention of the Parthians, but these were still open enemies in 32. There is a finished incisiveness about the lines that better fits the later period, but a final decision between the dates can hardly be made. The first epode contains a definite statement that Maecenas is going to the war and that Horace will refuse to remain at home if his friend goes. He is an indifferent soldier and can be of little service, he says, but the anxiety if he remained would be more than he could endure.

Horace, it is now generally agreed, went to the war and was present at the battle of Actium. At any rate the allusions found in two curious poems—the ninth epode [18] and the seventh ode—seem to be most readily explicable on this hypothesis. The epode has not a single good line or phrase though it presents an interesting picture. "When shall we have the Caecuban jar, Maecenas, that you have stored to celebrate Caesar's victory? The Galatian cavalry have abandoned the enemy and are cheering the name of Caesar. The Egyptian fleet still hides in the harbor. The enemy are donning the garb of mourning. Soon we shall see them making off for the shores of Crete or Africa. Bring cups to help us quell the sea-sickness!" Plutarch tells us that Octavian's fleet rode the storm for four days outside the harbor of Actium waiting for Antony and Cleopatra to offer battle,[14] and shortly before the battle the Galatian horse deserted to Octavian. We seem, therefore, to have a dinner scene on one of Octavian's vessels during those days of waiting, and the poet has been called upon to respond to a toast. Evidently Horace's muse was a poor sailor, but he kept the verses, perhaps in memory of the occasion.

The seventh ode, written, however, in epodic form, seems to have been composed at about the same time. Plancus, who never was satisfied, is complaining over the delays of the battle. He had special cause to long for a speedy victory, since as a renegade from Antony, he would surely meet death in case of defeat. He was apparently grumbling because he had not remained at his palace at Tivoli, or taken up his retreat in one of the famous cities of Greece. Horace, who loves his Tivoli as much as Plancus, writes him this consolatory ode. "Rhodes, Mitylene, Corinth and the rest are famous cities, and yet not comparable with your Tivoli with its water-sprayed gardens. However, take cheer, wars do not last forever, and whether you are in camp or destined to return home you may remember Teucer who kept up his good cheer even in exile." The theme, fitted to the weak character of Plancus, is petty enough, but the situation has some interest, the pictures of Tivoli are delightful, and the ringing vigor of the last lines keeps the poem in the reading list.

There is only one other poem which connects definitely with Actium, the song of victory, *Nunc est bibendum;* and it is written somewhat later than we should expect, because it took some time for Horace's return home and for definite news of Cleopatra's death to reach him. It has been pointed out that the first line may well be a reference to the epode written at the time of tedious anxiety before the battle when he asked impatiently for the celebration. Be that as it may, *Nunc est bibendum,* intended for a larger public, rises to its theme. It is noticeable that Horace does not mention the defeat of Antony—it is a defeat of Cleopatra and her Egyptian crew. But even so, the courageous suicide of the queen has touched him deeply and the last three stanzas become, somewhat surprisingly, a paean of praise for her:

> Deliberata morte ferocior,
> Saevis Liburnis scilicet invidens,
>   Privata deduci superbo
>   Non humilis mulier triumpho.

He is not yet a chauvinist.

On his return to his life in the country after Actium, Horace prepared two rolls for publication, the second book of satires, and the book of epodes. His ten years of literary effort thus produced only three rolls, and half of this might well have been omitted. But in extenuation he could remind his critics that he was earning a living at an exacting office through a large part of the period. He had also begun to compose his odes, and to these he now turned his whole attention for several years. But the bulk of his offering, in any case, was not large.

It would be highly gratifying to be able to arrange the poems of the three books of odes chronologically so as to follow Horace's changes in topics and his advance in style, but that cannot be done except in the case of some ten of the poems. And in reviewing these ten, where chronology is possible, one arrives at the conclusion, I think, that his art had been well-nigh perfected before the year 30 B.C.— he was then thirty-five years of age—and that he was as liable to fall into nodding in the later as in the earlier poems of the group.

Without attempting for the present to establish dates or precedence it may be permissible to take up a group of lyrics that clearly belong to his Sabine period, in order to catch, if possible, what the new life is like which has called him from satire to song. One of the earliest is II, 13, which can be dated the year after Actium. The real theme is the glorification of Alcaeus and Sappho, whom he is now reading avidly as models of true lyric verse. He deliberately recommends Alcaeus as his favorite. A poet who has suffered the shocks that Horace had, and has spent ten years at writing satires, who has not attempted lyric verse until he is thirty-five years of age is obviously not likely to write ardent love lyrics. Alcaeus had been buffeted by storms as Horace had, and he spoke a language that Horace comprehended. This poem (II, 13), not wholly successful in Horace's usual technique of terseness and neat transitions, nevertheless reveals his favorite trick of avoiding obvious introductions and of teasing one on to the unexpected:

"A curse upon the malicious tree that all but crushed me. How near one can be to unexpected death, how near to the abode of the shades! how near to Sappho and Alcaeus, their songs, the spellbound throngs that listen, the music that turns hell into heaven!

In form this ode, as so many of the others, pretends to be a comment upon a chance experience, in substance a reflection of his reading. In spirit it is light and is intended to induce a smile of surprise.

Most of the Sabine pieces are similarly "occasional." We have mentioned III, 13, the *Fons Bandusia*. It purports to be a promise of an offering due on the morrow, the Fontanalia, the day of thanks to the sprite of springs. The rite is by no means merely an excuse for the picture. Whatever Horace's philosophy, he enters whole-heartedly, as we shall see, into the rites of his farm folk. He had grown up with such folk in his boyhood and his sympathy for the native cults was never lost. And yet in this ode it is the picture of that bursting spring beneath the ilex that he wants to etch in a vignette never to be forgotten.

> Fies nobilium tu quoque fontium,
> Me dicente cavis impositam ilicem
>   Saxis unde loquaces
>   Lymphae desiliunt tuae.

Let me add at once that the fashion of objecting to the picture of the sacrifice in the second stanza does strange violence to the tenets of criticism. Naturally the modern finds no beauty in blood sacrifice. But unless the reader is willing to project himself into the moods and creeds of the pagan writer he will do best to confine himself to twentieth-century poetry. I once met a traveller from India in the Brera—in that large room of seventeenth-century pictures of tortured St. Sebastians and

St. Catherines. Through his interpreter he asked what it all represented. "Is this your religion? How can men care to paint such gruesome scenes?" That Hindoo had been transported into a setting he was not prepared to comprehend. But we are hardly so far from pagan rites that similar comment on III, 13 can seem legitimate. The significant point is that Horace, the student of philosophy, could so readily become for a day a simple worshipper of the simple deities of his farm folk.

The same mood is illustrated in the exquisitely built *Faune Nympharum* (III, 18) written for the fifth of December when he shared with his tenants in the celebration to Faunus, including "his brother the ox" among the celebrants, and in the evening gave a dance to his heavy-footed neighbors. The twenty-second ode in the same book, a very brief dedication of eight lines to Diana, reveals him even more completely identifying himself with his farm folk. He had been hunting on the mountain, and had brought back a wild boar that had proved perilously savage. Following a very old and primitive peasant-rite, Horace dedicates to Diana the pine tree that stands above his house, and before this tree, now a visual embodiment of Diana, sacrifices the victim.

Imminens villae tua pinus esto,
Quam per exactos ego laetus annos
Verris obliquum meditantis ictum
    Sanguine donem.

His peasants who had been in the chase with him
understood that; they participated in the sacrifice
and in the good dinner that followed, and they smiled
approvingly.   That he put his simple prayer into
verse reveals how completely he could make himself
one with his people.   The moral worth of that naïve
faith to him and to them can hardly be questioned
after reading the 23rd poem of the third book,

Caelo supinas si tuleris manus,

where he has packed into five exquisite stanzas his
creed for the comforting of a peasant woman.

Fret not for costly victims, your Lares ask for
less.   On the ranges of Algidus grow the herds
for Rome's great sacrifice.   If the hand is guilt-
less that brings the offering, a handful of meal
and salt will win heaven's favor quite as well.

This is not affectation.   It may be Horace's boyhood
spirit conjured back, it may be poetic sympathy that
temporarily transforms an atomist into a *contadino*.
Be it what it may these verses are an authentic expression of something genuinely Italic, something
that the people of Rome had by this time very nearly

lost. The roots of that religion lay of course in a primitive animism which was outmoded in the city. In the hills, however, Faunus, the spirit of the spring and of the pine tree and the Lares of the crossroads and fields still lived. They were not resurrected as were the waxlike "nymphs" of the pseudo-classic poets of the eighteenth century. They played behind the trees on the hills above his house as they had on Voltur in his boyhood and they still heeded prayers. It delighted Horace to get back into communion with them again. And they rescued the poet in him—almost too late.

In reviewing the work of Horace's first ten years at Rome—before the period of the odes—we are amazed to find only the most casual references to Octavian who towered above all in the daily thoughts and conversation of the city, the ruler in whose interest even Maecenas worked night and day. This is significant because the court policy at Rome for many years had been to instill into the people the doctrine of the divine origin and the divine rights of this young ruler. And the poets in Maecenas' circle would naturally serve as the mouth-piece of this doctrine. Yet not one hint comes from Horace in all these years. And this is the more strange because later when the court decided to abandon the doctrine as inconsistent with the forms of the new constitution, Horace carried his laudation of Augustus very far. In a word, he is heterodox throughout his life on this theme.

In attempting to interpret Horace's course, however, much rests on a clear comprehension of the courtly theory. Julius Caesar had accepted the view of regal power which every king of the civilized world held in his day, namely that proof of divine right alone justified the disregard of a constitution and the imposition of autocracy. On no other basis would a ruler dare suppress popular legislation. Caesar had accordingly encouraged his courtiers to place his statue in the temples among the gods and heroes, and this, indeed, was one of the chief causes of the conspiracy against him among the nobles. At Caesar's death Octavian was not yet nineteen years of age. He had been chosen by Caesar as his heir to power, and yet he found himself neglected and despised. He saw that his strongest hold with the old soldiers and the populace would lie in insisting upon the divine claims of Caesar, for that would make Caesar's testament a sacred document, and his own claims to position both legal and sacred. The idea did not meet with much favor, and it probably hurt him in the eyes of the nobility as much as it aided him with the soldiers, but he persisted in furthering the doctrine. As soon as a strange fortune of war gave him the opportunity to seize the consulship at twenty, and through that to become one of the triumvirs, he compelled the senate to recognize Caesar as divine, and he began the building of a temple to him on the most conspicuous site in the forum. He was still only one of three, but he intended in time to be the sole ruler. And he had learned from Caesar that sole rule must be based upon the doctrine of *dei gratia*. After Philippi the doctrine was not strongly stressed. But Antony, now living in Egypt with Cleopatra, who was recognized as a divinity by her people, naturally accepted divine titles and honors. The provincials of the East, in Syria and Asia, were accustomed to the theory and expected their sovereign to hold himself as more than human. Octavian could not in theory consider himself inferior, though he dared not assert his claim with dangerous reiteration at Rome. The temple of Divus Julius and the statue of Caesar with divine attributes were in daily view and could be depended upon to keep the populace constantly reminded of Octavian's legacy. Literary references to the claim were expected. Vergil, who had been deeply devoted to Caesar, and from the first had acclaimed his heir, found nothing strange in the theory, for he had lived for years at Naples with a group of Orientals and Greeks who had been brought up on the

tradition. Vergil's Eclogues and Georgics take the
new phrases at face value, and it is probable that
most of the writers in Maecenas' circle did likewise.
But Horace did not. The spirit of Venusia and of
Philippi was still recusant. He was not yet ready
to believe liberty wholly dead and a triumvirate or
an autocracy the permanent solution.

It was probably a year or two of serious thinking
over the deep meaning of Actium which finally convinced him that the republic was no more and that
Octavian's régime could alone save the Roman world
from civil war. A triumvirate was impossible.
Lepidus had proved to be a weakling, and Antony
had very nearly succeeded in betraying a vast portion of the empire to Cleopatra and her children.
Octavian had demonstrated his worth. He was not
laboring for personal aggrandizement alone. He
saw more deeply than any one else into the needs of
the vast empire. He had called to his aid the best
men of the day and devoted his own days and nights
and theirs to laying a solid foundation of peace and
well-being for the newly reconstructed empire.
Horace saw that it would be mere stubbornness to
refuse hearty support to a man of such capacity and
wisdom.

But the interesting fact is that Horace when he
finally comes frankly forth with his acclaim after

more than ten years of silent brooding offers a doctrine of his own. He does not even now accept the
Oriental theory of divinity which Caesar had borrowed from Alexander and his successors at Antioch
and Alexandria, and which Octavian had played with
till Antony's course made it ridiculous. He adopts
the formula rather of the Greek Hero-cult, not entirely unknown at Rome to be sure, and yet not the
basic idea of Caesar's creed. Greek religion had
recognized the soul as surviving somehow about the
tomb and had demanded offerings to the dead on the
part of their descendants, somewhat in the same
manner as the religions of India and China to-day.
In the case of great men these rites were participated
in by the whole grateful community, and public
shrines were raised to such "Heroes." It was generally recognized that Hercules, Bacchus, Castor and
Pollux, for instance, had once lived upon earth as
humans, and shrines existed in numerous cities to
such kings as Peleus, Atreus, and Menelaus. In
southern Italy almost every Greek colony possessed a
shrine where offerings were made to the "Hero" who
had founded the colony. This view was not Roman,
but it was beginning to penetrate Rome through acquaintance with Greek customs and literature. Rome
had, before learning of the distinction, erected
shrines and temples to Hercules and Castor, but in

the Roman manner as to gods. It was only later that
they learned that these were not actually gods.
However as the custom penetrated, Romulus, the
mythical founder of Rome, was identified with the
old deity Quirinus, and Ennius, who was Greek in
training, spoke of Romulus as a "Hero." By Vergil's
day Aeneas had also been added to Romulus, at least
in literary references. The idea was now becoming
so familiar that even Cicero spoke of erecting a shrine
in the Greek fashion to his daughter Tullia. It is
significant that Julius Caesar's first step toward
deification took the form of a statue in the temple
of Quirinus-Romulus.

Horace from his early life in southern Italy was
of course familiar with the Greek practice, and became the more so from his life in Athens and his
compaigning in Macedonia and Asia Minor. When
he accepts Octavian as the inevitable master of Rome,
as the man who must alone bear the responsibility of
rule, he thereby admits that the constitutional republic is no more and that the man who holds the
position must be above the whim of the assembly.
To justify the theory of non-constitutional power
he conceived of the person of the ruler as a "Hero"
in the Greek sense, a hero who through his bene-
factions is entitled to the reverence and obedience of
the nation during life and to their worship after

death. He thereafter compares Augustus with the great benefactors like Hercules, Liber, Castor and Pollux (Ode I, 12), and as though to make the transition easier in Roman thought he also includes in his list a long line of Roman heroes: Romulus, Numa, even the Brutus who slew Tarquin, Cato, Regulus, Scaurus, the Paullus who fell at Cannae, Fabricius, Curius, Camillus, Marcellus and Julius Caesar. The list contains the names not only of successful military heroes but of good rebels against tyranny and great men defeated in noble causes. It is a strange assemblage and Octavian would hardly have been satisfied to identify his claims to godhead with the group of plain humans here juxtaposed.[15] But the poem gives the clue to Horace's own conception of Augustus' power. "If you will grant," he would say, "that the Greeks are justified in according reverence to their great benefactors, and if you will include our noblest men in such a list, I will gladly place Octavian in that list and include him among the immortals when his magnificent work is done. But I have given my definition. Read my phrases in the light of that." And henceforth, even after 27, when Octavian, now Augustus, decided that the Oriental theory had been too thoroughly shamed by Antony to be revived at Rome, and when he forbade shrines to be erected to himself in Italy, Horace consistently employs the "Hero"-formula which he had adopted. But he always uses it with reference to merit that deserves reverence, and at times the immortality which he prophesies is definitely the immortality merely of fame. Thus it is to be explained that while Vergil is always orthodox, accepting the theory of "divine rights" for the youthful Octavian, and suppressing it in 27 after the state had made its new decision, Horace is heterodox throughout, keeping silent until after Actium, and then, after the state's new decision, speaking repeatedly of the reverence due to Heroes who have done memorable service.

X

ODES, LYRICAL AND DIDACTIC

MANY of the odes—too many for our taste—are moral exhortations or examples of what might be called "Wisdom Literature." The Greeks and Romans had good historical reasons for respecting didactic verse. Poetry began before writing was known, and the earliest philosophers and teachers naturally versified their lectures so that they could the more readily be memorized and preserved. In fact there was in that day no formal composition in prose. Heraclitus' theories, Hesiod's *Works and Days,* Solon's wise saws were all in meter. The fashion continued to be respected throughout the Hellenistic period so that works on astronomy, agriculture, and local history were frequently put into verse, and the liberal statesman Cercidas, as we have learned from recent papyri, moralized in meliambi that may well have been known to Horace. At Rome Naevius and Ennius had written metrical Roman histories, Lucretius had written his *De Rerum Natura* in hexameters, and Vergil very recently his Georgics in the same measure. Some of Horace's most finished lines are to be found in these strings of axioms. The tenth ode of the second book is to-day a package of quotations:

> Rectius vives, Licini, neque altum
> Semper urgendo neque, dum procellas
> Cautus horrescis, nimium premendo
>   Litus iniquum.

> .   .   .   .   .   .

> Saepius ventis agitatur ingens
> Pinus, et celsae graviore casu
> Decidunt turres, feriuntque summos
>   Fulgura montis.

This ode is apparently addressed to Licinius Murena, the brother-in-law of Maecenas, who finally risked revolt and lost his head. At this time, however, he stood very near to power, and it might seem presumptuous of Horace to direct to him what can only be taken as a personal warning against undue ambition. But Horace occupied a privileged position and could take his mission as moral spokesman very seriously. There is no reason to suppose that he would hesitate to speak frankly, even to Murena.

Some of the other didactic odes seem to be merely an excuse for the insertion of a complimentary mention of a friend's name. We learn from Cicero's letters how prevalent the custom was of asking writers for the honor of a mention in their works,

and even Augustus asked Horace—with becoming
modesty—to be included among the persons he addressed in his epistles. It is not unlikely that Sal-
lustius, Tibullus, Dellius, Septimius, Valgius, Quinc-
tius, Postumus, and many others asked for similar
compliments, and that their names are fitted into
verse exercises that seemed to provide themes appropriate to the persons thus named. It is perfectly apparent that many of the didactic odes of the second
book were not inspired by a driving fire. Nevertheless, there are some of them that repeat the moral
themes of the satires with a zeal which is unmis-
takably authentic. Though Horace is now more frequently occupied with lighter themes, his moral con-
victions have not lost their edge. His invitation to
Maecenas (III, 29) to quit "the dust and din and
steam of town" for a while, to come out and see how
one can really live, contains as forceful a declaration
of his soul's independence as can be found. Dryden
has lost some of the incisive imagery in his translation but he has caught the power of the original in
many a line:

Happy the man—and happy he alone,—
　　He who can call to-day his own,
　　He who, secure within, can say
"To-morrow, do thy worst, for I have lived to-
　　　day:

Be fair or foul or rain or shine
The joys I have possessed in spite of Fate are mine,
   Not Heaven itself upon the Past has power,
But what has been, has been, and I have had my
      hour."

Fortune, that with malicious joy
   Does Man, her slave, oppress,
Proud of her office to destroy,
   Is seldom pleased to bless;
Still various and unconstant still,
   But with an inclination to be ill,
Promotes, degrades, delights in strife
   And makes a lottery of life.

I can enjoy her while she's kind,
   But when she dances in the wind,
And shakes the wings and will not stay,
   I puff the prostitute away.
The little or the much she gave is quietly resigned:
   Content with poverty my soul I arm,
   And Virtue, tho' in rags, will keep me warm.

      What is't to me,
Who never sail in her unfaithful sea,
   If storms arise and clouds grow black,
   If the mast split and threaten wrack?
Then let the greedy merchant fear
      For his ill-gotten gain,
And pray to gods that will not hear,
While the debating winds and billows bear
      His wealth into the main.

For me, secure from Fortune's blows,
Secure of what I cannot lose,
In my small pinnace I can sail,
Contemning all the blustering roar:
   And running with a merry gale
With friendly stars my safety seek
Within some little winding creek,
     And see the storm ashore.

His tirade against the lax social standards, in III, 24, *Intactis opulentior*, is the most bitter and effective of all his sermons. Not even in the period of his own distress did he so nearly approach a complete condemnation of capitalism and its consequences, and this ode comes very near being a challenge to the responsible ruler to meet his duty in social reform as he has in political organization. The poem is not hampered by a personal address. It is in general the old theme of irresponsible wealth being the root of all evil:

> aurum et inutile,
> Summi materiem mali.

At the end Horace gives hearty approval to Augustus' institution of a training school of *juvenes*—a kind of boys' scouts organization—which was meant to put young men through a severe cavalry and infantry drill at an age when they would be most likely to fall into vicious habits of life through idleness.

But he also calls for vigorous repressive legislation to be applied to more hardened sinners.

The cynicism of this ode may have sprung from a passing experience. The doctrine was not casual. The insistence upon the need of self-discipline in order to keep effective, of simple living in order to keep one's perspective, and of perspective in order to win the worth-while joys of living is not to be mistaken in these verses for mere fashionable padding. To Maecenas who knows him best Horace turns with the incisive remark: "You know that it is not over a dish of truffles that I preach plain living."

It is to Maecenas also that he addresses one of his frankest statements about himself, the sixteenth ode in the third book. As so often when he has a surprise in store for the reader, he begins in a disconcertingly casual tone off in the clouds. The personal reference does not come till line 18: "With reason did I shrink from raising my head to be seen afar";

> Iure perhorrui
> late conspicuum tollere verticem.

The whole ode [16] is, I think, a comment on a letter— not in the best of taste—which Augustus had written Maecenas asking that he send Horace to him to serve as his confidential secretary. This position was one of great distinction. It meant admission to the secrets of state and to a position of influence at the portal of imperial favors. It meant daily companionship with the inner court circle. Horace's qualifications were a practical training in the treasury office, an effective style in both Greek and Latin, demonstrated tact, and integrity. In order to place such an official in a position to meet the various members of that circle at his ease and—as later emperors found—to live secure from the possible temptation of accepting perilous favor from others, it was assumed that affluence must go with the office. There were estates in Africa, Asia, and Egypt that had fallen to the treasury during the war—such as had been assigned to Augustus' trusted helpers in lieu of pensions for life—and one of these could of course be set aside for Horace. We do not know the date of Augustus' letter but the reference to his palace as *regia* would best suit the period after Actium when Augustus was in Rome for two years, that is, in 29-27 B.C., when Horace was writing his odes.

It is Suetonius,[17] who later had access to the imperial archives, who has rescued a sentence from this letter. Maecenas is the recipient, and it was probably during the winter when Horace was spending some weeks with him: "Up to the present I have been able to conduct my own private correspondence; but now I am exceedingly busy and am none too well and I should like to deprive you of our friend Horace. Accordingly, he will come away from your table where he accepts your favors gratis [*parasitica*] to my palatial board and aid me in my correspondence." The future, *veniet*, is a royal command, and refusal must have been difficult for Maecenas as well as for Horace. Suetonius expresses some surprise that Augustus could condone rejection. We may suppose that Maecenas with his usual tact quelled his own resentment at the command and presented to Augustus the claims of literature which Augustus' order so cavalierly disregarded. Horace seems to have seen the letter, for the ode in question shows that he had felt the full force of the phrase *parasitica mensa*. The ode begins with a cynical interpretation of the Danaë myth that is quite out of harmony with the poet's usual reverence. "Jupiter resorted to gold when he wished to seduce Danaë. King Philip could capture any city to which a pack-mule could carry a bribe. Apparently gold can purchase anything." Then comes the sudden point: "Maecenas, you who are the glory of the humbler rank, I was right in refusing high office. Stripped of worldly goods, I am a fugitive from the house of wealth and seek the tents of the poor. With my rivulet, my woods, and my few acres, I am happier than the lord of African estates, though he knows it not. I have no herds and vineyards but I am not a pauper [this is the answer to *parasitica*]; you have given me all I need. Happiness comes as quickly by subtracting from 'I want' as by adding to 'I have.'" That was his great renunciation—not so difficult after all to Horace. But Rome doubtless learned of it and estimated it in the way Rome would, by the acres won or lost, and to the Romans therefore his moral odes were something more than versified Stoic precepts.

It has been said [18] that the adoption of the old Alcaic convention of addressing specific persons and choosing subject-matter from incidents and occasions deprived Horace of lyrical themes and kept him too objective for a song writer. One finds in him, to be sure, a guiding convention, but that it limited his range any more than a similar habit in Wordsworth, for instance, may well be doubted. The convention never was considered a law that he feared to break. The limitation of themes that we find in the odes was probably a matter of temperament, experience and choice. Unlike Catullus and Propertius, Horace did not begin to write at an age when passion dominates. He was thirty-five before he definitely turned to *carmina*—and it must be remembered that in

Italy youth matures early, and that in a pagan civilization, where restraint is not one of the cardinal virtues, deromanticising experiences may bring early disillusionment. And no sooner had the poet reached the age when young men apply the sphygmograph to the emotional pulse than he leaped into a gruelling war with two years of hard campaigns and a dismaying defeat. And this was followed by the loss of his fortune that seemed to preclude all possibility of pursuing his chosen career in literature and to force him into a dull settling down to years of drudgery. By then Horace had learned to quell his own emotions, to distrust his hopes, to smile with patient sympathy when others took their personal loves in all seriousness. He had reached a turn in his writing when the eternal verities of mature experience seemed more worthy of attention and when the forms of artistic expression interested him more than temporary moods. He had decided that art alone was abiding and to that he would devote himself.

It would of course be quite incorrect to suggest that Horace, like a few modern poets, had decided that the theme of love had been overdone and that other themes must have their due. Love had not yet, in point of fact, gained supremacy in literature, except in the verses of Catullus and a few of his followers, and these writers in the eyes of the mature

Horace were somewhat eccentric. He should be regarded not as a man who refused to follow Catullus but as one who saw no reason for going out of his way to follow him. The Lesbia poems, apart from their metrical form, he might have admired for their forceful simplicity of style, were it not for an un-Roman lack of reticence in them on a subject that no longer appealed to him; while the epic and elegiac narratives would bore him as precious.

Horace's own love-poems, if we may call them such, are accordingly studies in light and shade, in contrasts between fancy and actuality, in experiences remembered through the mist of time, or recalled by a Greek epigram, or by a friend's discomfiture, or by a passing mood. They pretend to no depth, not even to the incisiveness of cynicism. His own experiences are far enough away so that he can recall them in the best of humor, and in his choice of form he is particularly fond of a good-natured surprise, an unexpected conclusion.

The *Integer vitae* (I, 22) is typical. It begins mock-solemnly with phrases that are usually associated with stoic moralizing, but that also occur in erotic poetry to express the loyalty and integrity of love. The reader may proceed for several lines without suspecting its true intentions, but on reaching Fuscus, known as a joker from the ninth Satire, he will begin to detect a *double entendre*. The third stanza brings a laugh and the preposterous logic of the rest continues the fun to the end:

"The man who is *integer vitae, scelerisque purus* need fear no javelins or poisoned darts in desert wastes or dark forests. Proof: in my mountain woods, while singing of Lalage, I met unarmed a mighty wolf: he turned and fled. Henceforth, whether I must go to the steppes of Russia or to the African Sahara, I shall be true to Lalage."

In III, 11 also Horace deludes the reader through half the poem for the sake of telling the charming story of Hypermnestra, the *splendide mendax:*

"Mercury, teach me a song that can win the soul of the wilful Lyde, who refuses me. You once could charm the very rocks, even Cerberus, Ixion, the Danaids—yes, that is the very song she needs: tell her of the punishment of those Danaids who refused to love, and tell her of the one maiden who was true to her lover—sing her tale to the end."

Lyde of course is lost long before the conclusion, but one is not expected to miss her.

Quis multa gracilis (I, 5), a very carefully chiselled intaglio, is on the conventional theme of love's inconstancy, a theme found more than once in the Greek anthology. The poet's wise smile very nearly purses his lips, but not quite. The papyri of Egypt will probably provide us with more epigrams on the same subject, with the same metaphor, and the same cool sympathy, but it is safe to conjecture that Pyrrha will not be superseded. The sixteenth ode, *O matre pulcra filia pulcrior*, plays with mock-heroics as *Integer vitae* with mock-stoicism. It would be a pity to take it as an allegory, as so many would have us do. Whether it grew out of an incident—and it might well fit Metella, the daughter of Clodia—or a remembered suggestion does not matter. Horace is more concerned with the craftsmanship than with the reconciliation which he pretends to wish; and the chisel runs true.

The nineteenth ode,

> urit grata protervitas
> et voltus nimium lubricus adspici,

comes from the same studio, the retreat near the Bandusian fountain, miles away from experience, one may well believe. *Vitas hinnuleo me similis, Chloe*, (I, 23) brought the poet no tears. The rustling approach of Spring interests him more than *tempestiva Chloe*. *Barine* (II, 8) may contain memories of his visit to Barium with Maecenas' party—mentioned in the fifth Satire—but if so he added not a little to his recollections. *Donec gratus eram tibi* (III, 9) purports to be a poet's experience, as *clarior* shows. He is chivalrous enough to let Lydia out-play him at every turn, and if the suggestion for the poem came from Greek epigram, that touch at least would be Horace's own contribution—and the incomparably neat finish of the poem. *Extremum Tanain* (III, 10) certainly recalls the standard Greek theme of the bolted door that will not open to the lover. The form even has a name, paraclausytheron, and the conventional ending is of course "Open soon or I must die." Horace here parodies cynically: "Open soon —or I shall go." It is doubtful whether he would have serenaded very late into the night before any of these doors.

It would require courage to weave these pretty verses into a biography. They suggest a wide range of realities and phantasies, "nights of sacred memories," "emotion recollected in tranquillity," visions of "lazy, laughing, languid Jenny," and of the "tangles of Neaera's hair," and some of the experiences are no more real than the eyes that materialize after a banquet with mellow Caecuban or from the rhythms of a Greek epigram. We inevitably over-moralize Horace because it is his more solemn work that invites interpretation and occupies a disproportionate space on the page. Of his lighter work, to which his readers turn first, there is not much to say. It is there and tells itself out in a

fragrance that fortunately escapes analysis. The
only real antidote to a biography of Horace, is
Horace himself. After turning over his serious
homilies it is as well to recall for a moment that he
was a normal pagan who, while intensely concerned
with rectitude and honor, had not yet heard of the
pledges to be taken by the knights of the Holy Grail.
Horace, on the theme of woman, is limited even
from the point of view of Roman life. When this
bachelor clubman, in one of his most sentimental re-
flections on death, reminds Postumus of the joys that
he must leave at the grave, he musters up enough
fancy to include in the list his *placens uxor*. We
speak of feminine diction; Horace could be culled
to advantage for devastating samples of bachelor
diction. The poem (II, 12) written to Maecenas,
when he was about to become a benedict, gives us
Horace's only certain picture of a woman of Roman
society, and to judge from this, Maecenas' establishment had not offered the poet very many opportunities for association with such women. His vocabulary, which he evidently intends to be quite
courtly, is for a Roman rather Neapolitan. She
dances too well, as Sallust had but recently said of
Sempronia. Or perhaps he is here also reflecting the
taste of his Etruscan patron. The ode was one of
Horace's earliest. One cannot help wishing that we

had another written ten years later, after Horace had attended the banquets of Maecenas married.

His poems to his friends are seldom so exquisitely turned as his lighter lyrics. As we have remarked, some of them bear the address merely by way of compliment, but not a few reflect the character of the recipient. Vergil is addressed in a dedicatory poem upon his departure to Greece (I, 3). That Horace's well-remembered term of endearment, *animae dimidium meae*, meant all it so well says is not insisted upon at length. But as the poet stands upon the shore recalling the perils that his friend may meet, the full meaning of the separation becomes clear to him and he makes us feel it.[19] In *Scriberis Vario* (I, 6) we see a stern admiral who was deeply revered, but at a becoming distance. For Agrippa the only appropriate praise is a confession of inability to praise adequately. To Pollio, honored like Vergil with a dedication (II, 1), the poet attributes a magnificent list of achievements, ending with reminders of scenes from his history which had just been issued. We are referred not only to scenes of Pollio's victories, but very deftly to passages that prove Pollio's aversion to civil bloodshed. Pompeius, his old comrade in arms (II, 7) is addressed in a letter of welcome that has not a little of the Italian exuberance of Catullus' greetings to his returning comrades. The ode to Maecenas in ill health (II, 17) reflects the temperament of his friend as accurately as Seneca's long characterization. For his wealthy friend, Lamia, he adopts the mood of burlesque (III, 17). He invites himself to dinner. Lamia lives at Formiae, the old home of Lamos, the brigand chief in the Odyssey. Horace plays upon the similarity of names and concocts a genealogy as preposterous as one that would derive John Brown from King John:

"Lamia, you must be a descendant of the great Lamos who ruled the vast empire of Formiae, an empire at least ten miles in length. I'm coming to visit you to-morrow, but the raincrow forbodes storm. So go out betimes and gather in an armful of firewood for the roast pig you are going to serve me."

In inviting the magnificent Messala, his comrade of school days and Philippi, he wins his surprise by borrowing the august prayer-form from the ritual,[20] addressing his petition to the best cask of wine that he has (III, 21). In form, prayers are much the same the world over. Catullus' hymn to Diana best illustrates the usual form of pagan petition. The Roman suppliant named the god in reverent terms, his abiding place, and his parentage; then in praise recalled the attributes and great power of the deity,

and then at last he dared present his petition. Horace
addresses his jar of mellowest wine in all solemnity:

"Come, mellow jar, twin brother, born as I in
Manlius' consulship, be it brawls or fun or love or
sleep you hold in store, worthy of Messala, who
for all his wisdom honors you. You loose the
tongue, bring hope, courage, strength: come then,
and loves and graces with you, and the lamps shall
burn till dawn."

Few of Horace's actual prayers are addressed to
the great divinities of Rome. Presumably he was
not much given to praying. But there is one very
genuine prayer to Apollo, uttered apart at the dedication of the magnificent new temple on the Palatine
(I, 31). It has not the standard form, for it comes
at the close of the day when all the deep-voiced
priests had intoned their stately petitions in due form.
Horace was not pleased. They had spoken too much
like Roman dignitaries informing Apollo of the
magnificence of Rome, of her prosperity as proof
of her rectitude, and they had prayed in commanding
tones for even more material blessings. The poet
stood aside, withholding his Amen, and when the
unctuous procession had disappeared down the hill
into the Forum and he was left alone beholding the
glistening temple with its vast library—books for
him to delve in—he prayed meekly and fervently

not for lands and herds, not for the wealth that seemed to prove heaven's gracious indorsement, but for contentment with his lot and a lasting gift of song.

Finally—omitting much—we come to a group of poems called at times the "patriotic" or "Roman" odes. Horace's active participation in the civil war, his sixteenth epode written very early, his deep concern for the welfare of his country and its people, his associations with the inner circle of the court, these would all permit us to expect some political utterance at a time when policies of state were being thoroughly examined with a view to great administrative changes. Before Actium Octavian had laid down those triumviral powers which had made him an autocrat in his sphere of administration. When he returned in 29 he knew that he would soon be expected to decide on some plausible constitutional plan by which to continue to rule. for a complete restoration of the republic, which could only bring back civil contention, was not thought of. There were few precedents to follow in the desirable middle ground between autocracy and democracy. In settling the East after Actium Octavian had accepted divine honors in Egypt and Asia, for their peoples did not comprehend government that was not based upon absolutism. Would he carry this system westward as

Caesar had done and as he seems earlier to have intended? That would meet with criticism from the old nobles, who had taken deep offence at Antony's rôle as a divinity.

Octavian never decided things quickly. He kept control simply as consul until in 27 a decision was made. He offered to restore the constitution. The senate refused to give its approval. He then accepted proconsular power in the provinces in which standing armies were necessary, and was given the title of Augustus, "the revered." There was a republican basis for this proconsular position, and Augustus now definitely made clear—following the advice of Agrippa rather than of Maecenas—that he would have nothing to do with the Oriental type of monarchy but would follow Roman traditions. It was a decision of very great importance to all Rome, and the rejoicing was great.

To Horace these decisions must have brought genuine pleasure, and when we remember his silence during the preceding twelve years, when other writers had greeted Octavian as a divinity, we expect some grateful reference to this moderate decision. The first six odes of the third book are classed together with a solemn introduction that hints at a single purpose of high import. They were not written at the same time—in fact the composition of

them extends over a period of at least three years—
but in publishing them several years later Horace
wished to call attention to what he had said on
matters of state through that period of weighty discussion.

The sixth is perhaps the first of the group, a very
solemn and not too imaginative appeal for the restoration of religious faith and the good works that
go with it. It was composed after Actium and
clearly before Octavian began to restore the shattered cults in 28, that is probably in 29. It would
be too much to hold that Octavian acted upon Horace's advice, but Horace is doubtless one of the
effective spokesmen of the conservatives who had
for some years taken fright at the possible return of
Antony with Cleopatra, the consequent inundation
of eastern forms of worship and the eventual suf-
focation of old Roman religion and morals. The
fourth ode is difficult to comprehend. Perhaps it
was intended at first as a dedication to Octavian for
a book then in contemplation.[21] The first part concerns the poetic claims of the writer, the latter part
the magnificent work of the recipient, who has defeated the hordes of lawlessness and established the
rule of reason again. Having decided to withhold
publication for the time being, he later reworked
the intended dedication into an ode in honor of

Octavian and published it in the group of six "political" odes. That at least would be my explanation
of its peculiar form. The date is probably 29-28.
The theme of the first ode in the group is his favorite one of plain living, of the second, the stricter
discipline of youth memorably formulated in the
line *Dulce et decorum est pro patria mori.* We can
hardly date these two but they belong to the same
period.

In the third ode Horace warns us at the end that
he is interpreting Destiny. The poem has long been
a mystery, because the theme was considered too
serious for blunt language and because the poet resorted to the dramatic and solemn device of calling
upon Juno to speak in a prophetic utterance. We
cannot be sure of its date, but it seems to be Horace's
own interpretation of the theory of rule by grace
divine, his rejection of the Oriental-Caesarian formula, and his acceptance of a "Hero" revered because
of his deeds.[22] The date in that case would be 27,
that is, after Octavian had made his momentous decision and been honored with the title of Augustus.
Horace accepts and interprets this decision, and adds
apparently from his own reflection the theory of
immortality through merit. "Popular clamor will
not frighten *Justum et tenacem propositi virum.*
Through his deserts Augustus will reach the high

honor of the old 'Heroes.' This was the meaning of Juno's prophecy when she accepted Romulus as hero and promised her favor to Rome only on condition that Rome should be forever severed from Troy and all that Troy stood for." The reference to Troy is now generally taken to be an allusion to the old proposal of Julius Caesar's to move the capital of the empire to "ancestral" Troy or Alexandria as a first step toward the establishment of absolutism and divine kingship. Antony, following Caesar, had almost succeeded in making Alexandria the capital, a fact which Rome would not soon forget. These lines, therefore, are simply a grateful acknowledgment in symbolic language of Augustus' decision to build the empire on traditional Roman forms and not on an Oriental absolutism. It is one of Horace's most significant and elaborate poems.

The fifth ode, belonging to about the same period, is very nearly as serious in purport. Bound up with the problem of imperial policy was the question of how far the new régime should follow Julius Caesar's policy of expansion. Absolutism is necessarily based upon militarism, if for no other reason than that the army on which it rests must be fruitfully occupied. Britain, invaded by Caesar, had been neglected, and the Parthians were still after twenty-five years unpunished for their victory over

Crassus; meanwhile the defeated soldiers of Crassus were still living in disgraceful captivity. Horace does not express himself on the main issue of whether war shall be resumed,[23] but out of the discussion he borrows a text and contrasts the low morale of the soldiers that surrendered with the superb sacrifice of Regulus who refused to be ransomed after capture because he feared the establishment of a dangerous precedent. The speech of Regulus is expressed in tense, staccato clauses; and its power is felt the more because of the controlled pathos of the following lines that describe his deliberate departure to certain death. For its complete realization of an heroic character at the intense moment of self-sacrifice this ode stands alone. But for this ode it might indeed be possible to deny Horace rank among the great lyric poets.

These six odes show clearly enough that Horace was not merely a silent bystander while great questions of state were being discussed. He was intensely concerned, and while we need not suppose that Augustus—now a very powerful man—asked for Horace's advice nor indeed altered his views to accord with it, we see that Horace in the sixth ode at least anticipated and urged a serious reform, that in others, when he approved of the wise course pursued, he not only could aid progress by giving support in pithy utterance, but that he had, as in the third, his own independent point of view on policies that needed adoption.

We have discussed only a small number of the odes, choosing here and there illustrations of typical themes and methods of composition, and those only for the purpose of getting a more intimate acquaintance with the poet. By the year twenty-three B.C. Horace had a collection that sufficed for three normal rolls, and he accordingly shaped them up for publication. There must now be introductions and epilogues. The whole collection was to be dedicated to Maecenas, and Horace does this gracefully if conventionally. "Many are the occupations of men. I have chosen to sing, because that is my great joy. And if you, my patron, shall find that this is poetry, that will suffice." After the first poem there follow in positions of honor one to Augustus, an old one at that, then one to Vergil, then one to Sestius, the consul of the year. The second book is dedicated to Pollio, while the third has the six political odes at the forefront with a new opening stanza to bind them together, the famous lines beginning:

Odi profanum volgus et arceo.

Augustus is not honored with any dedication. It is difficult to say why. Perhaps Horace feared to incur the charge of presumption, or possibly he was not wholly at ease over the new turn the government had taken in the year 23 in the direction of a permanent monarchy.

The epilogues are more interesting, in their progress from the amusing assumption of diffidence in the first to the confident assertion of lasting accomplishment in the third. They were of course written at the same time while he was editing the rolls for publication. Horace had been writing lyrics for seven years, had read many of them to his friends and had received much praise. He was fairly sure of their quality—and his was the first considerable body of lyric verse in Latin. How would the volumes be greeted? At the end of the first book we find only the two quiet deprecating stanzas beginning *Persicos odi, puer, apparatus,* addressed to his slave who is waiting to bring in the congratulatory bouquets (of course).

No, my lad, never mind the roses and laurel wreathes. Just a sprig of myrtle, and we'll drink to the book here in the shade, you and I alone.

When the reader finishes the second book he finds the poet hinting at immortality in a suggestion intended only to draw a smile: Horace was now gray and growing uncomfortably stout and the picture of himself turning into the conventional bird of immortality struck him as a fair joke. As so often, he takes us off our guard by beginning with customary phrases. "Maecenas, this bard of yours whom you have loved, will soon depart to heaven on the wings of a swan. See, my legs are growing scrawny and my locks have turned white. But no weeping please —and no long procession when I'm gone."

But at the end of the third book, the serious mood returns. Horace knows the worth of his work and he is no longer going to risk misunderstanding by deceptive depreciation. Forestalling criticism of arrogance by using a phrase of Pindar, he wrote the bold lines that have come to be the accepted epilogue of generations of poets:

Exegi monumentum aere perennius . . .

In that last poem Horace makes the claim that he first brought Aeolian song to Rome. The phrase seems to have been misunderstood by his readers, for in an epistle written soon after (I, 19)—when he had grown somewhat peevish over the critics and reviewers—he says more explicitly that he was not an imitator in his substance and his themes; he had modelled his rhythms on Alcaeus and that was all. This statement has been questioned by modern critics on two counts. In the first place it seems to

slight Catullus and the neoterics.   Horace is perhaps unjust, but from his point of view he was not
wholly wrong.   Even Quintilian does not speak of
Catullus as a lyric poet.   The truth is that both these
men were following a classification according to
genres and not according to content.   Catullus certainly wrote authentic lyrics, though not many, but
he wrote them in the meters of occasional verse, of
invective and epigram.   And the Romans thought of
him in such groupings.   Real lyrics, if one disre-
gards the music hall songs of Alexandria, were known
from the old Greek poets, and according to theory
they ought to be in the standard rhythms.   Catullus
had used the Sapphic lyric verse in only two poems,
both of a personal nature.   That was so slight a performance from the technical point of view that
Horace was justified in disregarding them.   Had
Catullus followed the norm he would not thus have
been passed over as a "lyrical" poet.

The second criticism directed against Horace's
claim concerns his assumption of originality, his insistence that it was form alone that he got from
Alcaeus.   If we take the trouble to watch Horace's
method of work I think we shall find that here too
we are wrong in questioning his statement.   We happen to know of several instances in which Horace
translated or paraphrased Alcaeus for a stanza or two,

but the striking fact has apparently not been noticed
that in doing so he had a specific formal reason for
his "imitation," and that he did not translate except
in the few instances where he had such a purpose.[24]
In introducing new meters to Rome which might not
readily be recognized at first reading he made it a
practice—so far as we can judge from extant orig-
inals—to base the first poem written in each new
meter on a well-known Alcaic poem which would
accordingly give the clue to the meter.   When
Horace began to write lyrics, the Romans, so far as
we know, had no verse in these forms except the two
Catullian poems in Sapphics, and one in the greater
Asclepiadic line.   Horace seems to have thought that
his readers might have difficulty in catching his
rhythms.   To be sure Horace's stanzas are very
regular, and any intelligent reader would soon
identify the rhythm by giving careful attention to
the quantities.   But the strong stress accent of Latin
might here and there tend to throw the reader off
the beat, the uneven lines of the stanzas might confuse readers unused to strophic verse, and the values
of the "irrational longs" and of the pauses were not
wholly matters of course.   Some readers might be
grateful for assistance.   It is probable that most
educated Romans had read such lyrics in Greek while
studying at Athens or under the tutelage of Greek

teachers at Rome. It would be natural, therefore, when he wrote in a Greek meter not hitherto freely used in Latin to refer to some well-known model. On papyrus rolls footnotes of reference were not customary nor was the Medieval method of adding a marginal note naming the meter. Horace's method of reference seems to have been this: the first time that a verse form occurs in his collection (except of course in the two dedicatory odes which had to be original) he seems to have referred to the correct meter by making the opening lines an unmistakable translation or paraphrase of some well-known Greek poem in that meter.

The first poem in Horace's collection that is written in his favorite Alcaic strophe is number nine, *Vides ut alta stet nive candidum*. We have six of the first eight lines of the original of this poem in Alcaeus (Bergk's edition, fragment 34). Horace's paraphrase is so close to the original that any cultured reader would recognize the source, and he would thereby have the clue to the meter. In the rest of his ode Horace has developed his theme on his own lines, and he has even risked consistency of setting by doing so. It is therefore doubtful whether he would have referred to Alcaeus at all had he not needed to direct his reader to the verse form which he was here introducing. Horace uses this strophe in thirty-seven odes and in only one other, I, 37, *Nunc est bibendum,* does he use this device. This ode is chronologically one of his earliest lyrics, probably the first one composed in Alcaics, and we may assume that in writing it he felt the need of directing his readers to the correct meter. If so his device was invented at the very beginning of his career as a songwriter.

The first poem of the collection in the Sapphic hendecasyllabic strophe (with the exception of the second dedicatory ode) is Carmen 10, *Mercuri facunde nepos Atlantis.* Here too the same device is used. We still possess three Sapphic lines of Alcaeus' original in his hymn to Hermes (Bergk, fragment 5). This poem was well known, for it was the first poem in the Alcaic rolls written in this meter, and it was the very poem which Hephaestion also cited as his example of the Sapphic. Horace's paraphrase is apparently not this time as close as in the preceding case, but the identity of title would give the reader the appropriate hint and Porphyrio says explicitly "hymnus est in Mercurium ab Alcaeo lyrico poeta."

The only poem that Horace has left us in the Ionic meter is number III, 12, *Miserarumst neque amori.* The model for this both in theme and meter was Alcaeus' poem of which we have a line in fragment 59. Again the model was well known for it is the poem which Hephaestion cites as his standard example of this meter.

The greater Asclepiadic meter Horace used only twice in his first three books, in I, 11, *Tu ne quaesieris,* and in 18. In both of these instances—since the meter was unusual—he seems to have directed the reader to Alcaic poems written in the same meter. In the case of number 18 there has never been any doubt that the original was Alcaeus, fragment 44, which was casually quoted by Athenaeus. In number 11 there is some doubt, but fragment 41 of Alcaeus gives the gist of Horace's concluding lines and this seems to be his model.

These poems include all the instances in which Horace is known to have borrowed both theme and meter from Alcaeus and in all of these the principle that we have suggested holds good. Numbers 9, 10, 11 of book I and III, 12 are first occurrences of a strophe in the collection, except for the dedications. Number 18 is in a rare meter, and 37 is a very early ode. There are only two other lyric meters, the lesser Asclepiadic and the greater Sapphic in Horace's book of odes, and similar models for these will doubtless come to light as new Alcaic papyri are found. In view of the fact that for none of the other 98 poems of Horace can models be found that supply both theme and meter the principle seems to me to be established.

As regards the lesser Asclepiadic line, Horace used this in his dedication to Maecenas. A model for a personal dedication probably did not exist in Alcaeus, and such a model could hardly have been used had one existed. It is noteworthy that Horace avoids an intricate strophe here. Perhaps he uses the verse stichically simply because he has not yet indicated a model and intends the repetition of the line to disclose the rhythm. However, in the third ode where it is used in a stanza we should expect a reference to an Alcaic original. The theme occurs in the glyconic propempticon of Callimachus, fragment 114, and this is usually considered Horace's model. This theory is inviting since the glyconic line would provide Horace's reader with the rhythm for his first line—whereas the second line was already known from the first ode. Nevertheless, in view of Horace's regular practice elsewhere and in view of his reiterated statement that he modeled his rhythms on Alcaeus we may surmise that Alcaeus probably provided the pattern in theme as well as in form for Horace's propempticon, that Alcaeus wrote a propempticon in the "first Asclepiadic strophe," and that Callimachus and Horace both employed that as model. For the so-called greater Sapphic

(Horace I, 8), we have as yet no Greek parallel, but Plautus, *Most.* 149, indicates a common Greek source, and since I, 8 is the first occurrence in Horace of this meter we may, in view of Horace's usual practice, feel confident that somewhere in Alcaeus' rolls there was a poem on this theme composed in this meter.

Except for these poems where guideposts to the meters were deliberately used, there are very few odes that can be called imitative even in the modern sense. These few usually have a *raison d'être* in the use of literary association for some special effect. *O navis referent* (I, 14) is at once seen to be an allegory by those who recall the original of the first lines; in the address to the bolted door (III, 10)— an old theme that poets liked to play with—the amusing surprise at the end becomes more effective because of suggestions from the standard type; drinking songs and "steamer letters" belong to all ages and need hardly be considered mimetic, while the last epilogue, *Exegi monumentum*, speaks with a self-assurance that craves and obtains justification by reminding the reader of Pindar's self-commendation. These are not instances of imitation. We may, therefore, accept Horace's statement of his purpose and achievement as entirely satisfactory. In originality he ranks with Alcaeus; in breadth, humanity, and artistry he is, if we may judge Alcaeus from the poems and fragments that have survived, at least his peer, and in the Roman odes III, 5, and IV, 4 there is an exaltation that carries the mind beyond Alcaeus to Pindar.

XI

EPISTLES AND LITERARY THEORY

FOR a few years following upon the publication of
the odes Horace lived much on his farm writing
epistles in leisurely fashion, and these epistles contain a few personal references that deserve mention
in a biography. The thirteenth seems in fact to be
a letter accompanying his presentation copy of some
work of his to Augustus, a trifle that is more interesting for the reply it fetched than for its contents.
It is put in the form of instructions to the slave or
freedman who is to bear the book: he must carry
the enormous load carefully, he must not disturb the
busy prince at the wrong moment, he must bow
deferentially and present the gift graciously. He
calls his servant Asina, which is apparently a play on
his real name of Onysius. Suetonius later found a
copy of Augustus' letter of thanks and quotes the
following sally:[25] "Onysius has brought me your
book, for which I thank you, though it apologizes for
its brevity. You are apparently afraid that your
books may be longer than their author. Though you
are not tall, you do not lack in girth; my suggestion

is that you diminish the page so as to extend the roll and make it as plump as you yourself are." Perhaps Augustus' chief interest in poetry was in "quantity-production." He doubtless wished the poets to make his reign a distinct artistic success. In any case he went so far as to give Horace what he must have considered a very gracious invitation to call: "Please avail yourself of the hospitality of my home as though you were my guest. This you may well do with propriety and without presumption since I have asked that I might enjoy this intimacy if your health permitted" (a reference apparently to his previous offer of the secretaryship). The letter was as cordial as Augustus could make it, but it was after all not an invitation one would care to accept. A little more generous perhaps is the tone of another passage quoted by Suetonius: "How much I have you in mind you may learn from Septimius, our mutual friend, for I happened to speak of you in his presence. And even if your pride has kept you from being my friend, I have not for that reason withdrawn into silence." One wonders whether Augustus had not after all penetrated into the true interpretation of Horace's ode to Maecenas, the *Inclusam Danaen.*

The most personal letter in the first book of epistles is the 19th, addressed to Maecenas, and concerned with the reception of the odes. Maecenas had consoled Horace on the unfavorable comments of the critics by asking "why is it men criticize the odes in public while all the world is reading them with delight?" Maecenas had also referred to various unkind remarks about the poet's dependence upon Alcaeus, which Horace had brought upon himself by his epilogue. The answer shows that Horace was as sensitive to the "chorus of indolent reviewers" as poets usually are. It is almost peevish, but very illuminating: "As I introduced the Archilochian iambic in form—certainly not in substance—so too I employed the Alcaic verse—but only the rhythm. Did not Alcaeus himself adopt the verse form of his predecessors? Is that imitation? If you wish to see what real imitation is, behold these men who have now taken to writing Horatian odes. They even ask for my brand of wine, and would drink vinegar if I did. Why do they criticize, you ask. Because I don't read my verses publicly and ask for their criticism." We do not know whether Valerius Cato still lived. Probably not. But his criteria of poetry still held in many of the school-rooms, and there the strictly classical work of Horace had come with a shock. It would take a few years before Roman taste was disciplined into accepting his standards. Had Horace issued his poems singly or in small editions the critics would have been better prepared to understand his aims when the complete volumes came. As it was the poems in a few years established their supremacy. Before issuing his fourth book of odes Horace was conscious of the fact that he had been accepted as Rome's poet: *et jam dente minus mordeor invido.*

The first book of epistles contains many of his most delightful compositions. The epistolary form was of course not his invention, but it is the Horatian epistle that has dominated the type in later literature. Here again, as in the satires, we find a progression in form concomitant with a mellowing of mood which is more important as a determining factor in his compositions than models. Just as the poet began using the Lucilian satirical medley and at once in his first book of satires subordinated the personal lampoon to the requirements of his theme, then in his second book adopted the dialogue or *sermo* as a special type of the medley because of its didactic convenience, so here in his maturity he adopts still another form which is even more malleable and adapted to a wide range of literary, ethical and social comment. He includes a few epistles which might well have been personal missives in prose, probably in order to keep up the illusion of reality. But these are of course brief and well selected. Some comment or joke or nicety of style worthy of wider attention these also contain. The very brief letter of introduction to the crabbed "heir-apparent" Tiberius in favor of Septimius (no. 9) is a model of exquisite phrasing.

> sed timui mea ne finxisse minora putarer,
> dissimulator opis propriae, mihi commodus uni:
> sic ego maioris fugiens opprobria culpae
> frontis ad urbanae descendi praemia.

Is there another passage in Latin so carefully written? After reading Tacitus on Tiberius it is enlightening to go back to this reflection of the young man's character written to him thirty-five years before he became emperor. Dr. Johnson might have turned that into English; I shall not attempt it. Numbers 3, 8, and 16 are epistles to absent friends, two of them at least on the staff of Tiberius in the east, *comites* of a man of state as Catullus and Cinna had been. The position of *comes* had come to be recognized as a kind of travelling fellowship for poets in search of inspiration and copy. Recognition and tactful advice from the now distinguished poet was, we can see, much valued by the young literati.

The fourth epistle was sent to the poet Tibullus, who belonged to Messala's circle. It reveals Horace's open-hearted friendliness to a younger man who devoted his time to elegies, a genre that never appealed to him. Tibullus was apparently not well, indeed he died in the year 19, soon after this book of epistles appeared. The tenth letter argues with Fuscus against his devotion to "Fleet Street," and, with a peculiarly modern use of the word *natura*, in favor of a life "according to nature." Country life, he thinks, gives perspective and teaches a lesson in true proportion. The fourteenth is like it, but suits its tone to the poet's overseer who had been imported from the city rabble. Horace does not here pretend to adopt a moral tone that would over-shoot the mark:

Nec lusisse pudet, sed non incidere ludum.

The sixteenth, also suggested by the same theme, though addressed to a man who can catch a higher pitch, combines good old Sabine conviction with Stoic maxim and the religion of Euripides, the sum of which he gives in the familiar line:

Oderunt peccare boni, virtutis amore.

The second epistle is sent to Lollius, a young lad who is still at his studies. It points out what Plato had failed to see, a fact observed later by the critics of Plato and reiterated by them to save a favorite poet—that Homer by implication is a very good textbook in ethics. After reading the second book

of Epistles one cannot be too sure that Horace himself held very firmly to this didactic function of
Homer. But perhaps Lollius needed some such inducement to draw him away from the practical education to which he was being submitted.

The sixth epistle, the famous *Nil admirari*, has
been called an enigma, and to judge from the variety
of interpretations found in the recent commentaries
made for school boys, it still is. This is a case where
Horace assumes that the recipient, Numicius, and
the general reader know his point of view so well
that he may venture a sarcasm without a label.
Sellar, for instance, seems to assume that Horace,
after advocating complete philosophic calm, continues
with the doctrine that any pursuit (the search for
wealth, political honor, love or what not), provided
it is engaged in with all one's energies, has salvation
in it. And that is the common interpretation. But
nowhere has Horace entertained such a doctrine.
Surely Horace is here advocating a life of philosophic
poise and tranquillity as against the feverish struggle
for the goals set by Roman society. The clue is
given at the end: *hi* refers to Horace's own well-
known insistence upon self-control (found in lines
1-31), *isti* to Numicius' "go-getting" creed (in lines
31-66). The careful reader will see that the alterna-

tives offered by Numicius are all brought to a re-
ductio ad absurdum, except the last which is the
Mimnermus-Propertius creed, and that, to Horace, is too ridiculous to need a label.   Indeed this
interpretation [26] was long ago given by Pope's paraphrase in the pointed couplet:

> Adieu—if this advice appear the worst,
> E'en take the counsel which I gave you first.

A word may be in place regarding the connotation
of the Horatian *Nil admirari*, the most perversely
mistranslated phrase in Horace.   Pope's "Not to ad-
mire" and Voltaire's character of "Poco Curante"
wrongly connected the phrase with Cyrenaic "in-
difference."   And the romantics, Shelley and Byron,
accept this interpretation with vengeful glee.   One
suspects that Shelley knowingly garbled when he
wrote to Peacock: "Nil admirari—which, I should
say, prope res est una to prevent there ever being
anything admirable in the world."   The original of
Horace's phrase had a more dignified setting in
Pythagoras, and its synonyms in Stoic and Epicurean
thought invited men to that composure which might
be attained only by philosophic employment and by
the knowledge of nature's laws.   Horace's develop-
ment of the theme and his illustrations show that to

him the phrase had the positive connotations of the more fully developed philosophy. His final comment on the subject is found at the end of the eighteenth epistle:

Sed satis est orare Iovem quae ponit et aufert,
Det vitam, det opes; aequom mi animum ipse parabo.

The seventh epistle is a revelatory letter to Maecenas who had asked Horace to return to Rome, and had somewhat tactlessly hinted at his obligations to his benefactor. Horace is evidently angered. "My debt to you is great and I gladly acknowledge it, but I am not as young as I was, and to care for my health I must remain away from Rome till spring. If this seems ingratitude, I will submit to your judgment and give back the estate. In the fable the fox lost his liberty by feeding too well in the corn-bin. Have I done so? Telemachus wisely refused the gifts of Menelaus which he could not properly use. There is also a story of a tradesman of Rome who accepted from a patron an estate which destroyed his happiness. He saw his mistake and gave back the gift. The moral is obvious." Horace does not remind Maecenas that after all his Sabine farm was only a fair return for the home which the state had confiscated, but he doubtless wrote with that thought in mind. Horace's pride, of which Augustus had complained, was not a thing for any one, not even Maecenas, to disregard. The publication of this frank epistle is proof enough that Maecenas was the kind of sportsman who could appreciate the poet's temper.

The twentieth epistle is an epilogue of the sort that was now coming into frequent use. Since books were copied by hand it was possible that owners might add matter of interest to them. Furthermore if the label were lost a book might in time pass without signature. An appropriate epilogue would therefore prevent misunderstanding as to the author, the date, and the original contents. In this one, which contains the usual personal references, we learn that the book was issued in the year 20, three years after the publication of the odes.

Horace lived twelve years after the publication of this book of epistles, and after Vergil's death in 19 B.C. Horace was recognized as the foremost of Rome's literary men. Augustus called upon him to write the choral song for the septi-centennial celebration in 17 B.C., and in 15 it was he who wrote the odes of victory in honor of Tiberius and Drusus. Nevertheless it is misleading to apply to him the designation of "poet laureate." He is not now, and never was, the real spokesman of Augustus. Had he been so considered we should have a longer list of poems upon themes that deeply concerned Augustus —elegies, for instance, on the death of Marcellus and of Agrippa, and especially poems written to support the drastic moral reforms of Augustus that were shaped under intense discussion during the years just preceding the great celebration. It is quite possible that behind what Augustus chose to call Horace's pride there was still some feeling of distrust of a régime which claimed to have "restored the republic" while in practice devitalizing republican institutions by keeping them in innocuous desuetude. And we may also add that after the execution of Murena in 22, Maecenas, while still a loyal supporter and helper of the prince, was not as before the indispensable counsellor of state. For such reasons, if for no others, political discussions seem henceforth to be less vividly reflected in Horace's writings. The poet seems also to be taking longer vacations from work, and to be permitting himself to think that the moments of inspiration come less frequently.

A rather long and casual epistle to Florus which is placed as the second epistle of the second book and which apparently belongs to about 19 B.C., reflects this spirit of diffidence. He is no longer writing lyrics and excuses himself with a string of irrelevant pretexts which he intends to be taken as a transparent veil for laziness. The epistle is dull, but contains several interesting facts about his early life, a good line here and there, and a significant allusion to the young elegist, Propertius. This reference comes in his criticism of the general practice of poets who recite their compositions and form mutual admiration cliques.[27]

> My friend writes elegies, and I write odes:
> O how we puff each other! " 'Tis divine;
> The Muses had a hand in every line."
> Remark our swagger as we pass the dome
> Built to receive the future bards of Rome;
> Then follow us and listen what we say,
> How each by turns awards and takes the bay.
> Like Samnite fencers, with elaborate art
> We hit in tierce to be hit back in quart.
> I'm dubbed Alcaeus, and retire in force:
> And who is he? Callimachus of course:
> Or, if 'tis not enough, I bid him rise
> Mimnermus, and he swells to twice his size.

Propertius who called himself the Roman Callimachus and acknowledged the influence of Mimnermus must be the person indicated. This poet, though he had now been writing for ten years, and was early received into Maecenas' circle, is not once explicitly mentioned by Horace, the most generous of men, nor does Propertius mention Horace. This itself would be enough to indicate a standing difference between them, which could readily enough be explained by the very striking disparity in their temperaments. When in the sixth epistle, written a few years earlier, Horace took occasion to show the absurdity of various vulgar assumptions, he thus refers with scorn to what we have termed the Propertius-Mimnermus view:

> Si, Mimnermus uti censet, sine amore iocisque
> Nil est iucundum, vivas in amore iocisque!

That indicates the temperamental antithesis between the two men, for the reference to Propertius can hardly be doubted. But of course the divergence extended also to critical theories, a more serious matter. Propertius deliberately proclaimed himself the successor of the Hellenistic poets in Greece and of the neoterics in Latin (II, 34, 87).

> Haec quoque lascivi cantarunt scripta Catulli,
>   Lesbia quis ipsa notior est Helena.
> Haec etiam docti confessa est pagina Calvi,
>   cum caneret miserae funera Quintiliae,
> et modo formosa quam multa Lycoride Gallus
>   mortuus inferna vulnera lavit aqua.

The three poets here mentioned are the very ones from whose themes and style Horace would claim most widely to depart. Every principle of composition which he later lays down in the *Ars Poetica* is evidence of his aversion to those tendencies of the neoterics which Propertius illustrates. Even in this second epistle the nature of his objection to them is revealed by the fact that he immediately follows the passage which is quoted above by demanding merciless patience in artistry and the use of every effort to attain a rich and pure Latin diction.

Horace's next datable composition is the *Carmen Saeculare* written in 17 B.C. at imperial request for the great celebration of Rome's founding. As we have learned from the inscribed record of this three-day festival, an important item was a choral song which was sung by twenty-seven boys and twenty-seven girls in the area in front of the new Apollo temple. The inscription also has the item: *Q. Horatius Flaccus carmen composuit*. The seventy-six lines of Horace's hymn afford us little pleasure to-day. They are of course merely the words for a prayer-hymn that gained whatever ceremonial charm it may have had from the music and from the rhythmic movements of the choral groups. Furthermore the high priest must have given the poet the substance of the prayers to be set to verse, for in such matters Roman religion was very exacting, and the precise sacred phrases, the proper mingling of praise and petition, could not be left to the untrained. The contents, therefore, are more welcome to the student of religious ceremonial than to the reader in search of poetry.

We are unfortunately not informed regarding the division of the verses between the two groups of singers, a detail that might aid the imagination in restoring the ceremony. There is, however, one novelty in the treatment of the Sapphic rhythm here which may perhaps give the clue. Hitherto Horace has regularly used a strong rhythmic pause after the verse stress of the third foot. In this poem he frequently uses a pause one syllable later, which mellows the line because it removes the emphasis of the stress at the center and gives a falling rhythm there as at the line end. The effect is one which Vergil was fond of using in his hexameters in the Dido-scenes of the fourth book of the Aeneid. My suggestion is that in the stanzas sung by the boys alone the strong stress is always given by means of the "masculine" caesura, whereas the new fluid form occurs in the stanzas sung by the maidens and in the choral parts in which maidens have a share. The contents of the stanzas can apparently aid in determining the division of the stanzas between those two groups.[28] I should, therefore, divide the stanzas as follows:

1 2	} full chorus	Proodos: address to Apollo and Diana.

3	youths	Prayer to Sol-Apollo.
4-5	maidens	Prayer to Ilithyia-Diana.
6-7-8	youths	Prosper Rome through the next saeculum!

9-10-11	{ antiphonal { couplets }	To Apollo and Diana.

12	youths	May Jupiter and Juno prosper
13	maidens	citizens and ruler.
14-15-16	full chorus	Song of joy: the age of peace returns.
17	youths	Prayer to Apollo.
18	maidens	Prayer to Diana.

19	full chorus	Epodos: the gods have heard our prayers.

Whether or no this division is correct, the contents prove that some such plan was used to make the execution a very pleasing performance. And we have a reference in the sixth ode of the fourth book which shows that Horace was free at least to plan the evolutions of the chorus and to train the singers, —and that he enjoyed the task.

With this "laureate" work should be compared the odes of victory in honor of Tiberius (IV, 14) and Drusus (IV, 4) after the brilliant campaign that brought safety to Italy's northern boundary and

pushed the frontier beyond the Alps. In that campaign Drusus forced the Brenner Pass, followed the
river Adige up into the Voralberg and at Lake Con-
stance met his brother who had struck eastward from
the Rhine. The ode to Tiberius shows the effect of
an uncongenial subject. Tiberius was a good soldier,
but not an inspiring theme for poetry. Drusus fares
better, though Pindaric imagery and Livia's prosaic
hints seem to obtrude. However the latter half of
the ode is a brilliant epinicion that ranks with Horace's best works. The other odes of the fourth
book, occasional pieces mostly, some being rejected
odes refurbished to fill space, cannot be dated with
certainty, but there is nothing to indicate that any
were written after the death of Agrippa.

A literary epistle to Augustus (numbered II, 1)
seems to have been written about 14-13 B.C. to judge
from a reference to the new altars erected to Augustus at that time. Augustus, who was absent from
Rome the greater part of the years between 21 and
13, seems now to have been impressed by the fact
that although Horace had addressed epistles to many
of his friends there was none addressed to him. He
wrote to Horace specifically requesting one. The
letter, with its assumed modesty and somewhat con-
strained deference, similar in tone to the several
letters written to Horace after the early one in which

Augustus had made the mistake of using a command, may have occasioned some slight impatience in the poet, but he had only his own over-sensitive pride to thank for being spoken to thus by the emperor. "I would have you know," writes Augustus, "that I am deeply offended because you have not especially addressed to me any of your several compositions in this manner. Is it because you are afraid that it might disgrace you hereafter if it should appear that you were my intimate friend?" Augustus of course was not always so prim, and he wished only to be of service to literature, but his phrases invited an over-elaborate deference in return, the usual Horatian assignment of Augustus to the rank of "Hero." Fortunately this attitude wears off in an introduction of seventeen lines, after which the poet runs along at his usual ease. He seizes the opportunity, so appropriately offered, of inviting the emperor to become interested in poetry, and specifically in contemporaneous poetry. "Conscious of our great past we over-estimate our early authors, Ennius, Plautus, Accius and Lucilius, who were after all but careless writers, whereas only now is Rome's literary group laying enough stress on artistic finish; a review of our literature from the native Fescennine play will explain why the old poets were slipshod. Poetry does deserve attention, since it gives profit as well as pleasure, and it needs encouragement because it is a very difficult art. Fortunately the emperor has patronized poetry and has had the great reward of seeing men like Vergil and Varius respond to his encouragement." It was timely doctrine—especially since Augustus had asked for advice.

The assault upon the early poets may seem bitter, and it has been compared with the attack made by Pope and Dryden upon everything from Chaucer to Shakespeare. In point of fact Pope was encouraged by this epistle of Horace to write his tirades. A comparison, however, is not fair. Horace did not attack his superiors, and his charge is not based upon lack of "modernity" but rather upon the slipshod work, haste and avidity of the older writers. He knows the Roman proneness to blind conservatism, and he knows how much he had himself lost by being kept too long at studying the crude works of Livius Andronicus. His commendation of the Augustan group, even if it seems not disinterested, was a service that needed performing.

His brief sketch of early Roman literature in this epistle is wholly incorrect. The error, however, did not spring from a desire to wrench history into didactic service, as seems to have been the case with Pope. Long before this time Accius had shaped the history of Roman literature upon incorrect lines by failing to carry his researches far enough, and Horace's teacher Orbilius, as school masters will, had apparently read antiquated lecture notes to his boys. The essential corrections had already been made before Horace wrote this letter, for they are mentioned by Cicero in his *Brutus,* but Horace had been in Athens at the time and apparently had missed them. The amusing thing is that Pope, paraphrasing Horace's mistake, wrenched the story of English literature to fit the mistake.

There is also another passage in this epistle which need not be taken too seriously, the poet's insistence upon the utility of poetry. Horace is here addressing a powerful but busy and prosaic patron of letters. Why harm his case by keeping the appeal on too high a plane of art? "At most," he says cynically, "poetry is quite harmless and inexpensive, and keeps the author out of mischief; it is even useful in teaching children their ABCs, it occupies adults pleasantly and it provides good moral lessons!" We know that Horace held didactic verse in high esteem, but this passage in the Augustan epistle does not escape the suspicion that Horace had found the invitation of a Philistine prince oppressive. His effort to accommodate his phrases to the comprehension of his august emperor nearly plunged him into a betrayal of cynicism. The epistle is written in his best style and except for its sketch of literature is well worth reading.

The so-called *Ars Poetica*, which is really a letter to Piso and his two sons giving rather casual advice about verse-writing, seems to belong to the poet's last years, 10-8 B.C. This Piso, if we are to believe Porphyrio, was the son of Caesar's father-in-law.[29] Horace's letter is therefore written nearly fifty years after Catullus and Cicero lampooned Piso's father. This fact suggests a curious literary connection between the poets. Catullus' Piso was the patron of Philodemus, and it is from Philodemus' lectures on criticism that we have recently obtained a brief outline of the views of Neoptolemus which are supposed to have inspired Horace to write the *Ars Poetica*. One suspects that Horace may have written the book while a guest at Piso's villa at Herculaneum where he would have access to Philodemus' books of criticism.

Piso, like his father, was interested in poets. Two Greek epigrammatists, Antipater and Apollonides, have left verses in his honor. He had done some verse writing, and to judge from Horace's remarks, the sons—youths of about 18-21—were also poetasters. Horace seems to have no great enthusiasm for their compositions. Whenever he addresses them most directly it is to recommend further study of good models, more critical standards, and the advisability of withholding publication. It is a pity that the critical essay was not addressed to men of real talent. Had the Pisos been poets of great promise the letter might well have struck an entirely different note, urging self-reliance and the courage to launch out into original work. I do not mean to say that Horace would not have continued to preach the doctrine of classicism, but it is quite apparent that the thought of the Pisos does not inspire him with the faith and enthusiasm that might have made his essay a protreptic rather than an apotropaic sermon. The epistle must not be read as Horace's full expression of his poetic creed.

Before writing a long letter embodying critical advice—a new field for him—Horace would of course look over the standard books on the subject. Porphyrio says explicitly that Horace used Neoptolemus, a third century writer, as a guide. Perhaps he did. In any case textbooks on composition then as now, however much they differed in what to emphasize, contained chapters on all the standard themes; any one of them might serve to suggest the subjects that called for treatment. In Porphyrio's day—during the fifty years of civil wars that broke the empire—scholarship was at an extremely low ebb and books were rotting unused. It is not at all certain that Porphyrio happened upon the actual author that Horace used. Philodemus, in his poetics, discussed the precepts of Neoptolemus so that we know something about them.[30] After reading his discussion we may conclude that Horace had probably seen the book or something like it and that he diverged or added new points as frequently as he followed his guide. In fact we can still find more points of similarity between Horace's epistle and Aristotle or even between Horace and Cicero than we can between him and Neoptolemus. That is to say, ordinary critical rules had been standardized, and all intelligent men had at hand, as we have to-day, advice regarding clarity, brevity, force, form, meters, and all the rest. Horace knew the maxims, but what is more important, he had had a wide experience in composition, had been bitterly criticized, and had himself led in a vigorous movement toward what we call classical ideals. He never had subscribed to rules on any man's authority and he does not in this epistle. If here and there we find him summarizing standard precepts, it is because he had worked through practice to the discovery that those rules were valid. What he says in the *Ars Poetica* can be taken as his own conviction, narrowed down here and there to fit the capacities of the Pisos, who were typical Roman poetasters. Accordingly it seems legitimate to treat the work as Horace's running commentary on the literary experiences that he had lived through.

Horace begins with a severe attack upon poets who disregard unity in composition. Critics have been prone to regard the passage as a joust against windmills, for even Aristotle had long before stated the doctrine of "the beginning, the middle, and the end." However, the fact is that Horace lived in an age of literary aberrations when a re-emphasis of the simple law of unity was very much needed. Ennius, the father of Latin poetry, had issued his annals in triads and hexads. These were doubtless soundly proportioned units; but when the poem was issued as a whole it naturally failed to carry the impression of a well-constructed composition, so that his successors took the liberty of narrating unorganized history without regard for unity. But more insidious than this misread example of Ennius was the fondness for fine writing that Alexandrian romanticism had fostered at Rome in Horace's youth. If we possessed the miniature epics popular at the time we should know whose misplaced descriptions of woods and rainbows called forth the curse upon "purple patches" in the first paragraph. Readers have with good reason suggested that the "altar of Diana" is an allusion to the *Diana* of Valerius Cato, and that "flumen Rhenum" is similarly a reminder of the neoteric excrescences of Furius' epic on Caesar's conquests in Gaul. Horace's friends doubtless found references also to passages of poets like Calvus and Cinna in the other allusions. These men were of course the outstanding figures of the neoteric school of Catullus and Calvus when Horace began to write. As we noted in discussing them earlier, they performed a necessary task in training the eye to search for scenes of beauty in nature and in man's handiwork, for a deeper meaning in the old myths and for emotional significance. But in doing so they had allowed themselves, as the *Peleus and Thetis* of Catullus and the *Ciris* of Vergil prove, to become episodic and to forget the demands of form. The Horatian group had now successfully opposed this tendency, but it did no harm to impress the doctrine with some explicit examples. Vergil, who had in his youth followed Catullus, had later seen his error, and in the Aeneid had very carefully plotted out his story in a rational sequence of events. Horace too had observed the demands of unity in all his odes. To be sure, his codas are not obvious nor does his first line always give the key to the substance. His introductions, as we have seen, sometimes lead curiously to surprises, and his transitions are delicate enough to require close attention. Nevertheless illumination comes at the end, if not before, and the pattern clears up in reminiscence even if for a while it had seemed obscure. Some of his best effects he attained by insisting upon form. To Horace then the rule of unity was inexorable, and one of the great reforms of his group was its reintroduction into Roman poetry. His delightful remark, by the way, that lucid order is after all merely a matter of being full of one's subject is only one of the many indications in this essay that for him the intricate rules of textbooks were superfluous. We may add that the subject of unity could hardly have had the same prominence in Neoptolemus, if indeed that writer touched upon the question at all, for Neoptolemus lived before it had become the fashion to disregard the maxim.

There follows a paragraph on diction (lines 47-72). This subject had troubled many writers—Lucretius and Cicero, who had found the Latin vocabulary inadequate, the neoterics, who on the one hand had effectively used a colloquial Latin in their minor poems while on the other they had enlarged poetic diction in their epyllia, Valerius Cato, who had praised the use of Greek words in Lucilius, and Caesar and the Atticists, who had avoided bombast and called for pure Latin in forensic composition.

Such discussions of diction were of course very old. In the days of Neoptolemus they had centered chiefly about the claims of poetic diction and the propriety of using realistic colloquialisms in literature. Stoic teachers of rhetoric who had introduced the serious study of language were apt for that reason to be purists and their formal doctrine to some extent influenced the Roman Atticists. In Horace's day, this doctrine received much support from men like Varius, Quintilius and especially from orators like Pollio and Messala who carried on the Atticistic tradition. Horace was naturally a conservative, and in his youth he had severely criticized Lucilius and his commentator Cato from the point of view of a purist. But his experience had shown him the danger of limiting poetic vocabulary, and he had now come to feel that the repressive doctrine was going too far, especially in hampering the work of a poet like Vergil. Horace, therefore, throws his influence on the side of the liberals on this question, though his liberalism is well reasoned at every point. His advice is this. Since words wear out in usage, some effort has to be made to enlarge literary diction. One remedy is to give old words a new lease of life by breaking up clichés and refitting the words into suggestive associations. Horace's own works will supply many pages of striking collocations like

*splendide mendax, simplex munditiis, integer vitae,
dedecorum pretiosus emptor.* Another device that
he recommends is to study a foreign language—
which in his day meant Greek—and, when finding
concepts expressed there for which Latin has no
equivalents, to create out of Latin roots the words
that will express such concepts. That in fact was a
method already employed to advantage by Cicero
and Lucretius, to whom we owe a large part of our
vocabulary of abstract terms. Finally Horace warns
against allowing words to be abandoned too quickly
to the limbo of archaisms, and, since usage is the
final arbiter, against being too fastidious about ex-
pressive words found in daily colloquial usage. This
is all excellent doctrine and might to advantage be
adopted in the modern schoolroom; and here too we
must add that some of it at least could not have been
found in Neoptolemus since the method of enlarging one's diction by the use of a foreign language
could hardly have occurred to any one in his day.

There follows (73-88) a paragraph on the meters
appropriate to the various genres. The elegiac is
suited to sad themes and to epigram (the pointed
epigram of Martial was not yet), the iambic to invective, a stately iambic to tragic dialogue, certain
lyric meters to themes of praise and love,—and he
adds "if I do not know the temper and spirit of each

verse-form or if I ignore them, what right have I to
the name of poet?" "Mere red tape," insists Saints-
bury. But to Horace this was not mere red tape.
Every sane critic of his day felt that the Latin hexameter was in danger of being over-weighted and that
the lines of comedy failed in lightness because of the
burden of spondees imposed upon them by the
abundance of long syllables in Latin. These things
were thought to be more or less unavoidable. There
were evils, however—due to ignorance or to a refusal
to train the ear to the proper ethos of verse—which
Horace had more at heart. From the time of
Laevius, who had broken over all restraint in his
polymetra derived from a late Greek fashion, there
had been manifest at Rome a failure to observe not
only the conventions but even the proprieties. And
conventions do not go for naught in poetry. Even
in English Dryden's couplet and Milton's blank verse
have acquired certain associations that cannot be disregarded with impunity. There can be little doubt
that Horace, schooled in the Greek poets of the
great age, must have chafed under the innovations
of the "new school." Catullus must have been particularly exasperating. In his youth, a clever and
ambitionless versifier, he had spent his time writing
lampoons and *vers de société* in the meters of trifles.
After he met Lesbia an intense passion possessed his

verse, but he continued as we have seen to write in negligée, as it were, using hendecasyllables and halt-iambics. One can imagine that many readers were mystified by the most poignant of his songs written in scazons:

> Miser Catulle desinas ineptire!

In the eyes of Horace Catullus had disregarded the proprieties, and Horace, who knew the facts, was correct in calling his predecessors to task for abusing their privileges and disregarding the obligation to give ear to fitness and to study well-established conventions. Horace rightly or wrongly felt that the *neoteri* did not study verse technique with sufficient care, furthermore—and here he was largely right—that they disregarded a vital tradition in employing verse forms like the scazon and the elegiac for subject-matter that had not been associated with them.

The full importance of appropriate meters it is difficult for us to estimate, for we possess too few Greek lyrics and we know too little about the moods of ancient verse-forms to be capable of judging with precision. But it would not be going too far to add that verse based upon quantity—as we may judge from music, which is quantitative—shows more sensitiveness to metrical variety than verse based, like ours, upon stress alone. Moreover, our meters are so few and simple, and these few must do service for so wide a range of expression, that we are utterly unfit to appreciate the fine distinctions wrought by the great abundance of feet and cola in Greek and Latin verse. When the English trochee, for instance, must serve the purposes of elegy, satire, love songs, and heroic verse, it is evident that our trochee will not acquire an individual ethos. Metrical rules were therefore not red tape to Horace, though they might to some extent be so to us. In considering the work of his predecessors, then, Horace had unquestioned reason for asking: *Cur ego si nequeo ignoroque, poeta salutor?* It was with this fact in mind that he repeatedly made the proud claim that it was he who first introduced the true lyric measures to Rome. And this is another point in which Horace had more to say than Neoptolemus, for he was speaking to Romans who had not yet acquired an accurate feeling for a large number of the Greek rhythms.

Immediately after this passage we find a keen observation (line 99) which also was obviously not in Neoptolemus, since the basis of it is the theory of a material soul. The point Horace is making is an old one, that technical perfection is not enough in verse, it must also have the compelling charm of imaginative poetry. We are so made, physically, he says, that we can reach and stir the soul by physical compulsion. What he means is that since souls are atomic there is a direct contact between the nerve atoms and the atoms that convey emotions,—a modern would resort to the James-Lange theory. Hence what the dramatist truly feels the actor can reproduce in himself and in turn can compel the auditor to share with him. It is therefore necessary for the poet first to feel what he writes. Horace's psychology is not quite up to date, but he proves himself in deadly earnest and states a valid fact of criticism when he says:

> Format enim natura prius nos intus ad omnem
> fortunarum habitum.

The central portion of the *Ars Poetica* deals chiefly with the drama. Presumably the elder son of Piso was engaged in writing tragedy and especially satyr plays. The latter though popular in Sophocles' day had never been adopted by the Roman stage, but young men must have tried themselves out in this interesting form of the drama. The temptation would of course be to write broad farces and travesties when staging satyr plays, and Horace insists that they can have no literary value unless handled with delicacy and restraint. In this section of his letter he may have taken suggestions from Neoptolemus for there was apparently no Roman experience upon which to draw.

Most of the standard rules about tragedy—the number of acts and actors, the proper use of a chorus, how far it was legitimate to alter a semi-sacred myth, how far to help action with narrative, and the like— had been inferred from the actual drama by Aristotle and his successors. But when Horace was writing this letter the drama was undergoing new changes before his eyes and they called for comment. At best tragedy was faring badly. The crowds that attended the free performances given on Roman holidays might number twenty thousand. It was impossible to have good literary tragedies acted in such a way that these crowds could comprehend them. Indeed we hear of very few tragedies composed in Horace's lifetime. Extravaganzas and ballets were taking their place. Some twelve years before Horace wrote this epistle, Pylades, a Greek actor, had introduced the pantomime. While a group of singers sang extracts of some tragedy to the music of an orchestra, Pylades silently acted—or "danced," as they called it—the rôles. The performances resembled those now associated with the name of the Russian ballet. The spectacle was one that a large crowd could enjoy since they were not obliged to catch the spoken word or to tax the intellect in an effort to hold the plot. It met with instant success, and many writers began to cut, trim, and adapt old tragedies to make them available for this type of presentation.

It was accordingly only natural for a dramatist writing at that time to consider that a legitimate performance might never be given to his play. He knew that if he took the new style of presentation into consideration, made his choruses into independent songs, used arias, monologues, soliloquies, or simple dialogues as far as possible, extracts at least might have a chance of being produced. The result of this influence was what we finally find in Seneca's plays, rather static productions loaded with monologues, lyrical choruses, and rhetorical dialogues which would lend themselves to detached musical recitation with interpretative dancing. Ovid's *Medea* was probably the first play influenced by the direction which the pantomime was taking, and that play was written several years before Horace discussed the drama.

One may well comprehend what Horace's views would be of such a tragedy, for he was concerned not with amusing performances but with the rights of literature. When therefore he criticizes with some bitterness the tendency of his day to write dis-

junctive choral odes, to give music and scenery too
large a part and to neglect fine points of characterization, he is inveighing against allurements that are
being induced by the popularity of the pantomime.

There is only one other point in the epistle that I
shall select for comment and that is Horace's discussion of the function of poetry, a question which was
old in Aristotle's day and could still be discussed with
vehemence by Wordsworth, Coleridge and Keats.
In approaching the subject Horace is careful not to
instill a dangerous confidence in the theory of
"divine afflatus" when speaking to the Pisos. He
probably knew them too well. When he addresses
them directly, as in lines 267 and 292, he advises
hard work as more effective than sitting back and
waiting for inspiration. It probably was prudent
advice. But he believes in inspiration and before he
concludes he states the cruel fact that poetry will not
come without native power (409). Then he comes
directly to the question of what poetry should aim
to do. Plato, poet though he was, had long ago
threatened to drive Homer out of his ideal state because of the dubious morality of his epic; Aristotle,
the most prosaic of scientists, had on the other hand
stated that the poet's function was to give pleasure.
We know now that Neoptolemus believed that the
poet should both please and instruct. This was of

course a doctrine that Romans in general would accept. Cicero does so explicitly, and even Lucretius acknowledges that he employs the artifices of poetry in order to make his scientific concoction palatable. Horace's practice we have observed. Many of his odes were written purely to give delight, but he also made use of the ode for didactic purposes. His conclusion in the *Ars Poetica* is in accordance with his practice. He agrees with Neoptolemus in saying that a work of art may do both, but he would prefer to modify Neoptolemus' conclusion by saying that poetry may do either and that either will suffice.

It is, of course, apparent that the *Epistle to the Pisos* was not meant to be what later writers have chosen to call it, an "Art of Poetry." A standard treatise on that subject would have ranged over many matters that Horace did not even mention. For instance, the textbooks of his day had full discussions of the methods of attaining to each of the three stylistic types—the sublime, the austere, and the middle—and on the first of these alone "Longinus" wrote a treatise far longer than Horace's epistle and far more important. Horace hardly mentions that theme. Perhaps that is because his eye is here lowered to the level of the Pisos, on whom a sermon on sublimity would be lost, or because he is giving stylistic advice and, being a poet, he knows that poetic inspiration is not attained by rules. Having written the Regulus ode he must have been aware that there was no didactic recipe for such work. The epistle in fact must be considered a failure if regarded as an essay on criticism, and it did much harm to poets of the Renaissance who, enticed by the authority of Horace's name, took it for what it was not intended to be and canonized its rules. It contains very much common sense, and most of its maxims are still valid, but like all rules of composition they are of value chiefly as deterrents to the unimaginative. That, however, does not destroy the utility of Horace's epistle. Considering, as did Horace, that inspiration is beyond the reach of doctrine, considering also that before the age of Horace the besetting sin of Roman poets had been undisciplined style, the critic—whose duty it is to view every work in its setting of cause and purpose—will appreciate the opportuneness and the effectiveness of its doctrine. And finally, as a commentary on the literary aberrations of the day it is perhaps the most valuable document that the historian of this period now has.

The epistle was apparently Horace's last work, and the reader may be forgiven if he finds in its tempered cynicism a spirit of weariness that has begun to revert to the mood of the youthful satires. Horace indeed was probably not in good health. He had suffered much from illness, and that he needed care in his last years we may gather from the solicitous request which Maecenas on his death-bed made to Augustus to be mindful of the poet. Horace survived his patron only a few months. He died at the unripe age of fifty-seven and his ashes were buried on the Esquiline near the tomb of Maecenas.

English verse translations of Catullus are as unsatisfactory as German or French versions of the lyrics of Wordsworth or Keats. I have therefore studiously avoided quoting such translations, and have assumed that readers who have but little Latin may help their memories by using the prose paraphrases of Cornish in the Loeb Library.

The commentaries of Ellis, Merrill, Kroll and Benoist may be recommended, also the essays on Catullus found in Mackail's *Latin Literature,* Duff's *Literary History of Rome* and Wilamowitz; *Hellenistische Dichtung* II. The following books may also be consulted to advantage: Munro, *Criticisms and Elucidations of Catullus,* Harrington, *Catullus and his Influence,* Duckett, *Catullus in English Poetry,* Macnaghten, *The Poems of Catullus Done into English Verse.* For bibliography, see Schanz-Hosius, *Geschichte Röm. Lit.* I, p. 292 (1927).

1. Numerous votive inscriptions to Diana with reliefs of the goddess and her hunting dog have been found in the foothills of the Alps. An inscription at Verona shows that she was there also identified, as in Catullus, with the birth-goddess and with the moon. Recent excavations have disclosed near Este an important Venetian goddess, Rehtia, worshipped with offerings of staghorns, and doubtless identified with Diana, *Jour. Roman Anthrop.,* 1922, 212.

2. Nos. 9 and 12 indicate that Catullus knew Veranius before his Spanish journey, which seems to have been in 61, the year of Caesar's proconsulship in Spain. When Metellus died in March 59, Clodia had already deserted Catullus for Caelius. Catullus' arrival in Rome must therefore be placed as early as 62.

3. For Clodia, and other persons mentioned by Catullus, see the editions of Ellis, Benoist and Schmidt; Schwabe's *Quaestiones Catull.*, Munro's *Criticisms and Elucidations*, Pascal, *Poeti e Personaggi Catulliani*, Giri, in *Rivista Ind. Gr. It.*, 1922, 161 ff.

4. Cicero, *Ad Familiares*, V. 1 and 2.

5. Wilamowitz has some good remarks on Sappho's poem in *Sappho und Simonides*, 56 ff. The poem is to be found in "Longinus," *On the Sublime*, Ch. 8 (now in the Loeb Library).

6. See *Cicero and the Poetae Novi, Amer. Jour. Phil.*, 1919, 396 ff. Cicero refers to the young men as the *barbatuli* because of the new fashion adopted by them of deferring the first shave (as a sign of mourning for Catiline, perhaps). Cicero, *Ad Atticum*, I, 14 and 16, refers to the trial, also Plutarch, *Cicero*, 29.

7. See *Vergil's Apprenticeship*, in *Class. Philology*, 1920, 108 ff.

8. Cicero, *Brutus*, 283 ff.; *Amer. Jour. Phil.*, 1919, 413 ff. The fragments of Calvus' verse may be found in Morel, *Frag. Poet. Lat.*, p. 84 f.; they are discussed in Pascal, *Poeti e Personaggi*.

9. Cicero, *Ad Atticum* II, 3, written in Dec. 60.

10. Cicero, *Pro Caelio* gilds him generously; in his *Brutus*, 273, he speaks well of his style. See Pascal, *op. cit.*, 99 ff.

11. Huelsen, *Topographie*, III, 56, gives most of the geographical references by the use of which this residential region may be mapped out. The north side of the Palatine hill rises rather steeply from the house of the Vestals in the Forum. On the edge of the hill fifty feet above the Forum stood a few houses: Cicero's, a porticus of Catulus,

and the residences of Scaurus and Crassus. A narrow street
(Clivus Victoriae), the most aristocratic in Rome, divided
this row from a line of houses which apparently stood in
this order: Seius, Clodius, Metellus and Clodia, Lutatius
Catulus, Caelius. One reached this street by a steep ramp
which ascended behind the house of the Vestals from near
the steps of Castor's temple. A plan of this quarter would
look somewhat like this:

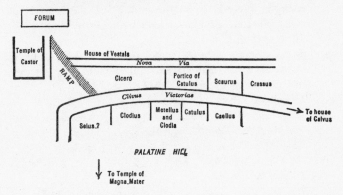

When Catullus in No. 39 refers to the 9th door-post from
Castor's temple as marking an unholy rendezvous he ap-
parently (counting two *pilae* to each hall-way) refers to
the house where Caelius lived. The chief references are
Seius (Cic., *de Domo*, 115), Clodius (ibid., 116), Metellus
(*Pro Cael.*, 59), Catulus (ibid.).

12. No two commentators agree about the interpretation of
68 b. The views expressed here are argued more fully in
Amer. Jour. Phil., 1914, 67 ff., and *Class. Quarterly*, 1926,
201. Pascal, *op. cit.*, 101 ff., discusses the Catullian epigrams on Caelius.

13. Discussed in *Amer. Jour. Phil.*, 1919, 409. The phrase
omnium patronus was apparently a compliment, see Cic.,
ad Fam., 6, 7, 4.

14. See *Amer. Jour. Phil.*, 1914, 67 ff., for a discussion of various interpretations.

15. Cic., *Ad Atticum* II, 12: *de lituis Boopidos.* Clodia is called the "trumpeter" of her brother's cohorts.

16. Cicero, *Pro Caelio*, 60.

17. Cicero, *Pro Caelio*, 36, candor huius te et proceritas, vultus oculique pepulerunt . . . (Caelius) calcitrat!

18. Cicero, *Ad Atticum* II, 24, Plutarch, *Caes.*, 14; *Amer. Jour, Phil.*, 1919, 405.

19. See Jacoby, in *Rhein. Mus.*, 60, 38 ff., Reitzenstein, *Epigram*, in Pauly-Wissowa, Mendell, *Class. Phil.*, 1922, p. 1 ff., Wheeler, *Catullus as an Elegist, Amer. Jour. Phil.*, 1915, 155 ff.

20. Suffenus seems to be Alfenus Varus, see *Class. Quarterly*, 1920, 160. Alfenus suggests "profit"; Suffenus is meant to suggest the opposite. Horace, *Sat.*, I, 3, 130, turns *Varus* into *Vafer*.

21. In *Vergil, A Biography*, 96 ff., I have proposed an interpretation for Vergil's sixth Eclogue. Horace speaks of Quintilius in *Ode* i, 24, and *Ars Poet.* 1, 438.

22. On Cinna, see Morel, *Frag. Poet. Lat.*, p. 87, and Pascal, *Poeti e Personaggi.*

23. On the Attis see Lafaye, *Catulle et ses modeles*, 82 ff., and Wilamowitz, *Hellenist. Dichtung*, II, 291 ff.

24. See the metrical treatise in *Oxyr. Papyri*, no. 210.

25. See Cicero, *Pro Caelio*, and the correspondence of the year 57-56.

26. Cicero, *In Pisonem*, 68-74, shows that Philodemus was with Piso in Macedonia. Friedrich, in his edition of Catullus, p. 228, proposed the identification. The bronzes from the Herculanian "Villa Pisonis," now in the Naples Museum, are largely busts of Hellenistic rulers, such as might have been found in Macedonia and Byzantium.

27. On these verses see Hack, in *Harvard Studies*, 1914.

28. On Arrius and Hirrus, see *Raccolta. Ramorino*, 1927, p. 157.

29. Suet. *Julius*, 73, "Caesar made it plain that Catullus' verses on Mamurra had left an indelible stain, but when the poet gave an explanation Caesar at once invited him to dinner

and continued as before an intimate friend of the poet's father."

30. Since Acme is a Greek, to whom favorable omens would fall on the right, I would propose to punctuate sinistra ut ante, in line 8, but sinistra, ut ante dextra, in line 17. See *Class. Quarterly*, 1926, 203.

31. Of Clodia's later history we have no direct information, but Cicero mentions a "Clodia" in the years 45-44 who may possibly be Lesbia. Cicero desires to buy a garden and Atticus informs him that "Clodia's garden" might be for sale (Att. 12, 38; 41; 47; 52; 13, 29; 14, 8). Twice Cicero refers to this person in connections where the train of thought implies that Metellus' wife is meant. In *Att.*, 12, 52, he mentions her in the same breath as Lentulus' divorce of Metella, presumably Clodia's daughter. In *Att.*, 14, 8, the mention of Cleopatra reminds him of Clodia. Naturally Cleopatra's name would recall to him the whole Egyptian affair of 57 and the defense of Caelius against Clodia's attacks. If we dare follow such faint trails we may surmise that Clodia lived on for many years in retirement.

32. See *Class. Review*, 1920, p. 49.

33. On the same principle I think 2 b a fragment of a poem which separated the two *passer* poems, 2 and 3, and I believe that 78 b is a fragment of a poem on Caelius that corresponds to 77.

34. This epigram was addressed to a Cornelius, probably Nepos. The inclusion of this useless epigram in the collection would readily be understood if we might assume that Cornelius Nepos was the man who edited and published Catullus after the poet's death.

35. See Wilamowitz, *Hell. Dichtung* II, 298 ff.; Lafaye, *op. cit.*, 140 ff.; Wheeler, *Proc. Brit. Class. Ass.* XVIII, 132 ff.

36. Munro, *Lucretius*, Note on III, 57. Lucretius' dedication to Memmius seems to have been written after the latter became proconsul, see *Class. Phil.*, 1919, p. 286.

37. Catullus' reference to Achilles' tomb in the Troad in line 368 may well be reminiscent of his visit to the region.

38. The matter is discussed in *Amer. Jour. Phil.*, 1927, p. 273.

TRANSITION

1. *On the Sublime*, ch. 44, Fyfe's trans., Loeb Library.
2. Calvus was dead when Cicero wrote the *Brutus*, in the spring of 46. Cicero's letter discussing Calvus (*ad Fam.*, XV, 21) was written late in 46. There he mentions his friendly exhortations to Calvus.
3. Münzer, *Adelsparteien*, p. 341, note. It should be noted that Cicero mentions Metella's divorce when speaking of Clodia in *Att.* 12, 52. See note 31, above.

NOTES ON HORACE

1. For biographical data see Stemplinger, *Horatius*, in Pauly-Wissowa. The most reliable commentaries are Kiessling-Heinze and Plessis-Lejay-Galletier. The Bennett-Fair-clough prose translation in the Loeb Library is recommended. *Horace, a New Interpretation*, by A. Y. Campbell, *Orazio Lirico*, by Pasquali, *Horace and his Influence*, by Grant Showerman, Shorey's edition of the Odes, and Morris' of the Satires and Epistles contain much of value. Again, verse-translations have seemed inadequate.
2. Horace, *Sat.*, I, 6.
3. See L. R. Taylor, *Horace's Equestrian Career*, *Amer. Jour. Phil.*, 1925, p. 161, and E. H. Haight, *Horace and his Art of Enjoyment*, p. 36.
4. See *Class. Phil.*, 1920, p. 24.
5. Sellar, *Horace and the Elegiac Poets*, p. 123.
6. One reads between the lines of *Sat.* I, 4, and the introduction of I, 10, which was later deleted. See also *Amer. Jour. Phil.*, 1925, p. 72. On Cato, see Hendrickson, *Horace and Valerius Cato*, in *Class. Phil.*, 1916, 249.
7. Pseudo-Acron, I (ed. Keller), p. 402. Vergil's enemies "Bavius and Maevius" may well be the same as the "Furius and Aurelius" frequently mentioned by Catullus. Heidel (*Class. Review*, XV, 215) seems to be correct in identifying Catullus' Furius with the well-known Furius Bibaculus. This Furius, born about 90 B.C., came from Cisalpine Gaul.

He wrote neoteric verses and epigrams against Caesar, then, won over to Caesar's party, he wrote a turgid epic on the conquest of Gaul. In Horace's day he reverted to the neoteric group associated with Valerius Cato, lampooned Augustus and was repeatedly satirized by Horace. He seems to be the dog of *Epode* 6, and therefore the "Bavius" (the barker) whom Vergil dislikes. Maevius, of *Epode* 10, a counterpart of *Epode* 6, may well be the "Aurelius" who in Catullus' day was the friend of Furius. The nickname seems to be derived from his appearance (*inaurata* pallidior statua, Cat., 81, 4; cf. Horace, *Epode* 10, 16, *pallor luteus* of Maevius). This "Maevius" wrote verses on Metella (Porph. on Hor. *Sat.* II, 239) as did "Ticidas" (Ovid, *Trist.* II, 433) and it is not unlikely that the same man wrote under two different cryptonyms. In other words I suspect that the *Furius et Aurelius* of Catullus' poems, the Furius and Ticidas who later consorted with Valerius Cato (Suet., *de Gram.*, 4 and 11) and the *Bavius et Maevius*, who criticized Vergil and Horace, are the same *par ignobile fratrum*, on whom Domitius Marsus wrote his amusing epigram (Philarg. on Vergil, *Ecl.* III, 90). On Ticidas see *Class. Review*, 1920, 91.

8. Appian, *Bell. Civ.* V, 98, 99; Velleius, II, 79. The reference in Horace is, Ode III, 4, 28.

9. See Hendrickson, *Class. Phil.*, 1927, 46, *Amer. Jour. Phil.*, 1894, p. 4; Ullman, *Studies in Philology*, XVII, 379 ff.

10. Fiske, in the erudite tome, *Lucilius and Horace*, seems to me to have pursued an erroneous method and reached untenable conclusions.

11. Lugli, in *Monumenti Antichi*, 1926, 457 ff.

12. Campbell, *Horace*, p. 98.

13. See Heinze's introduction to the ninth epode, and Reitzenstein's comments on the seventh ode in *Rhein. Museum*, 1913, 256.

14. Plutarch, *Antony*, 66.

15. Drew has some pertinent remarks on this ode in *Class. Quarterly*, 1925, 159.

16. See *Class. Phil.*, 1925, p. 26.
17. Suetonius, ed. Roth, p. 297. This *vita Horati* actually appears anonymously in the MSS. of Horace's works, but the gist of it, including the quotations from Augustus' correspondence, is correctly attributed to Suetonius. However it seems also to contain gossipy insertions that belong to a later period.
18. Heinze, in *Neue Jahrbücher*, 1924, 153.
19. Hendrickson, in *Class. Journal*, III, p. 100.
20. Norden, *Agnostos Theos.*, p. 143.
21. See *Amer. Jour. Phil.*, 1921, 170.
22. It is just possible that this poem may belong to the year 22 when Augustus again refused to listen to a popular demand that he assume sole responsibility: see Cassius Dio, 54, 1. Ode I, 2 may also belong to Jan., 22 B.C. The last word, *Caesar*, seems to imply that Augustus might revert to Caesar's policy. Mr. Kenneth Scott has proved that there is no evidence for a cult of Augustus-Mercury.
23. Eduard Meyer's interesting interpretation of this ode (*Kleine Schriften* I, 454) goes counter to Horace's creed expressed in Ode I, 12. The story of Regulus which the poet uses here was not a myth: see *Class. Phil.*, 1926, p. 311.
24. See *Class. Phil.*, 1927, 291.
25. Suet., ed. Roth, p. 298. The name Onysius is facetiously taken as derived from Greek *onos*, hence Asina.
26. The excellent edition of Morris has the correct explanation.
27. The translation is Conington's.
28. See *Amer. Jour. Phil.*, 1921, 325.
29. Porphyrio's statement about this Piso has been doubted, but it still is more plausible than rival suggestions; Cichorius, *Römische Studien*, 337, and Art., *Licinius Crassus*, 73, in Pauly-Wissowa, XIII.
30. See Jensen's edition of Philodemus, Bk. II, Berlin, 1923. Jensen has overstated Horace's debt to Neoptolemus and underestimated the value of Philodemus. I am indebted to an unpublished essay by Miss Elizabeth Tappan for various observations on Neoptolemus.

INDEX